RURAL DEVELOPMENT

RURAL DEVELOPMENT

TADLOCK COWAN
AND
BRUCE E. FOOTE

Novinka Books
An imprint of Nova Science Publishers, Inc.
New York

For permission to use material from this book please contact us:
Telephone 631-231-7269; Fax 631-231-8175
Web Site: http://www.novapublishers.com

NOTICE TO THE READER

Library of Congress Cataloging-in-Publication Data:
Available Upon Request.

ISBN 13: 978-1-60021-161-4
ISBN:10: 1-60021-161-5

Published by Nova Science Publishers, Inc. ✤
New York

CONTENTS

PREFACE

In the post-World War II era, widespread rural poverty, most notably among farmers, dominated rural policy concerns. The Eisenhower Administration's Undersecretary for Agriculture, True D. Morse, began a rural development program in 1955 to assist low-income farmers. Because agriculture was the major economic activity in many rural areas of the time, a focus on farms and farm households became de facto rural policy. The war on poverty during the 1960s continued the focus on rural poverty as a central policy issue. When agriculture began to decline as rural America's dominant economic activity, policy attention shifted to rural revitalization. The 1980s farm financial crisis and economic dislocation in rural America brought the importance of rural structural change to the forefront of policy concerns. The further decline of farming to less than 8% of rural employment and the loss of many manufacturing jobs during the past decade have highlighted the growing gap between many rural areas and the Nation's urban/suburban areas. While no overarching framework guides rural policy at the federal level, adequate housing, employment creation and business retention, human capital concerns, poverty issues, medical care, and infrastructure development remain key foci of federal rural policy.

In: Rural Development   ISBN: 978-1-60021-161-4
Editors: T.Cowan, B.Foote, pp.1-44   © 2007 Nova Science Publishers, Inc.

Chapter 1

AN OVERVIEW OF USDA RURAL DEVELOPMENT PROGRAMS[*]

Tadlock Cowan

SUMMARY

More than 88 programs administered by 16 different federal agencies target rural economic development. The United States Department of Agriculture (USDA) administers the greatest number of rural development programs and has the highest average of program funds going directly to rural counties (approximately 50%). The Rural Development Policy Act of 1980 designated USDA as the lead federal agency for rural development. The Federal Crop Insurance Reform and Department of Agricultural Reorganization Act of 1994 created the Office of the Undersecretary for Rural Development and consolidated the rural development portfolio into four principal agencies responsible for USDA's mission area: Rural Housing Service, the Rural Business-Cooperative Service, the Rural Utilities Service, and the Office of Community Development. This report provides an overview of the various programs administered by these four USDA agencies, their authorizing legislation, program objectives, eligibility, and recent funding for each program. This report will be updated as events warrant.

---

[*] Excerpted from CRS Report RL31837, dated August 26, 2004.

U.S. RURAL POLICY: BACKGROUND

In the post-World War II era, widespread rural poverty, most notably among farmers, dominated rural policy concerns. The Eisenhower Administration's Undersecretary for Agriculture, True D. Morse, began a Rural Development Program in 1955 to assist low-income farmers. Because agriculture was the major economic activity in many rural areas of the time, a focus on farms and farm households became de facto rural policy. The War on Poverty during the 1960s continued the focus on rural poverty as a central policy issue. When agriculture began to decline as rural America's dominant economic activity, policy attention shifted to rural revitalization. The 1980s farm financial crisis and economic dislocation in rural America brought the importance of rural structural change to the forefront of policy concerns. The further decline of farming to less than 8% of rural employment and the loss of many manufacturing jobs during the past decade have highlighted the growing gap between many rural areas and the Nation's urban/suburban areas. While no overarching framework guides rural policy at the federal level, adequate housing, employment creation and business retention, human capital concerns, poverty issues, medical care, and infrastructure development remain key foci of federal rural policy.

Farming, and agriculture more generally, however, remain the major backdrop to much of congressional debate on rural policy. Since 1973, omnibus farm bills have included a rural development title. The most recent is Title VI of the Farm Security and Rural Investment Act of 2002 (P.L. 107-171). Agricultural issues are increasingly seen as part of global and regional restructuring issues which have significant implications for rural areas, especially in those where agriculture remains a dominant sector. Positioning rural areas to better compete in a global environment is one of the key issues framing much of the debate about the future of rural America. Omnibus farm bills have been the major modern legislative force for addressing many rural development issues.[1] While it is true that other legislation has significant implications for rural areas and rural residents (e.g., transportation initiatives, environmental regulation, finance and taxation, Medicare, Social Security), Congress has used periodic farm bills to address emerging rural issues as well as to reauthorize a wide range of rural programs administered by the various USDA rural development agencies. As the role of agriculture has continued to decline in rural economies, however, some are raising questions about the effectiveness of linking farm and rural policy. While the extent of overlap between federal agencies and programs targeting rural areas has been a concern noted by some rural policy observers, legislation enacted since 1990 reflects an effort to address rural issues more comprehensively.[2]

AUTHORIZING LEGISLATION FOR USDA RURAL DEVELOPMENT PROGRAMS

USDA's rural development mission is to enhance rural communities by targeting financial and technical resources to areas of greatest need. Three agencies, established by the Agricultural Reorganization Act of 1994 (P.L. 103-354), are responsible for the mission area: the Rural Housing Service (RHS), the Rural Business-Cooperative Service (RBS), and the Rural Utilities Service (RUS).[3] An Office of Community Development provides further community development support through USDA Rural Development's state offices. The mission area also administers the rural portion of the Empowerment Zones/Enterprise Communities Initiative and the National Rural Development Partnership.

Congress has enacted many public laws bearing on rural policies and rural residents. The Rural Electrification Act of 1936, to cite one significant example, was central to the provision of electrical power and telephone service throughout rural America. In 1966, Congress created the National Commission on Rural Poverty which published its famous report, *The People Left Behind*, the following year. Various loan and grant programs that target improvements in rural social welfare (e.g., housing) were also authorized and administered by the Farmers Home Administration (FmHA), the agency forerunner of today's USDA Office of Rural Development. Rural policy as an identified congressional concern, however, may be dated to the 1972 Rural Development Act, an amendment to the Consolidated Farmers Home Administration Act of 1961.[4]

New rural development legislation generally amends two authorizing statutes: (1) the Consolidated Farm and Rural Development Act of 1972 (P.L. 92-419) and (2) the Food, Agriculture, Conservation, and Trade Act of 1990 (P.L. 101-624). (Title III of the Consolidated Farmers Home Administration Act of 1961 was the original short title of this latter title, but the short title was re-designated the 1972 Act and is classified principally as

Title 7 U.S.C. Chapter 50, 1921 et seq.[5]). A brief description and overview of key sections of the basic statutory authority for rural development programs are provided below.

Rural Electrification Act of 1936 (7 U.S.C. 901 Et Seq.)

The act established the Rural Electrification Administration during the Great Depression to create jobs and electrify rural areas by providing subsidized loans and grants to rural electric cooperatives. In 1949, telephone cooperatives also were brought under the program. Cooperatives are a common form of business organization in rural areas, structured essentially as non-taxed entities owned by their users. In the 1930s, only a few farms and rural households had access to electricity; by the mid-1950s, the proportion of rural homes with electricity matched suburban penetration, and by 1975, more than 99% of all farms had electricity. Likewise, by the mid-1970s, telephone penetration in rural areas had topped 90% and it has held steady at roughly 95% of households for the past 20 years.

Title V Rural Development Act of 1972 (P.L. 92-419) (Title III of the Consolidated Farmers Home Administration Act of 1961 (P.L. 87-128), 7 U.S.C. 1926 Et Seq.)

This title is part of the Consolidated Farm and Rural Development Act of 1972 and is often referred to as the "ConAct." Title V directed the Secretary of Agriculture to provide leadership within the executive branch and to assume responsibility for coordinating a nationwide rural development program using the services of executive branch departments and agencies, including, but not limited to, the agencies, bureaus, offices, and services of the Department of Agriculture, in coordination with rural development programs of state and local governments. The act also authorized the Community Facility Loan program, the Rural Business and Industry Loan program, and the Rural Business Enterprise Grant program.

Rural Development Policy Act of 1980 (P.L. 96-355)

This legislation affirmed USDA as the lead agency for rural development. (The 1972 Act named USDA as the lead federal coordinator for rural policy). The act also added responsibilities to the 1972 Rural Development Act. It authorized the Secretary of Agriculture to expand the Department's leadership role through which multi-state, state, sub-state, and local rural development needs, plans, and recommendations can be received and assessed on a continuing basis.

Rural Economic Development Act of 1990 (Title XXIII of the Food, Agriculture, Conservation, and Trade Act of 1990 (P.L. 101-624))

Part of the omnibus 1990 farm bill. Title XXIII amended the Consolidated Farm and Rural Development Act of 1972 to establish in USDA the Rural Development Administration (RDA). Legislative action saw significant debate between House and Senate Appropriations Committees with the House Agriculture Committee over establishing the RDA. The newly formed RDA absorbed all non-farm FmHA functions. Important provisions include:

- Establishing (1) a Rural Partnerships Investment Board to provide lines of credit for rural economic development revolving funds; (2) (in the Department of the Treasury) the Rural Business Investment Fund; and (3) local revolving funds. Amended the Consolidated Farm and Rural Development Act *of 1972* to establish a delivery system for certain rural development programs;
- Providing water and waste facilities. Amended the Farm Credit Act of 1971 to authorize lending for water and waste projects and revised water and waste facility financing provisions. Established a rural wastewater treatment circuit rider program. Amended the Consolidated Farm and Rural Development Act to establish emergency community water assistance grants and water and waste facility loans and grants to alleviate health risks.
- Enhancing human resources. Provided for enhanced rural community access to advanced telecommunications. Amended the Consolidated Farm and Rural Development Act to authorize loans for business telecommunications partnerships and establish rural emergency assistance loans;
- Supporting rural business. Amended the Rural Electrification Act of 1936 to establish a technical assistance unit, defer economic

development loan payments, and establish the Rural Incubator Fund to promote rural economic development.

The Omnibus Budget Reconciliation Act of 1993 (P.L. 103-66)

Title VIII established the first rural Empowerment Zones and Enterprise Communities (EZ/EC). The EZ/EC program is a grant-making initiative whose objective is to revitalize low-income rural communities (and low-income urban areas) in ways that attract private sector investment. USDA administered the rural EZ/EC program and the Department of Housing and Urban Development administered the urban EZ/EC program. In December 1994, three rural Empowerment Zones (EZ) and 30 rural Enterprise Communities (EC) were named. The Taxpayers Relief Act of 1997 added two additional rural EZs and 10 more rural ECs. A third round of competition, authorized by the Consolidated Appropriations Act of 2001, created two more rural EZs.

Federal Crop Insurance Reform and Department of Agriculture Reorganization Act of 1994 (P.L. 103-354)

Title II authorized reorganization of the Department of Agriculture. It authorized the Secretary to establish the position of Under Secretary of Agriculture for Rural Economic and Community Development to succeed the Under Secretary of Agriculture for Small Community and Rural Development. The act further organized rural development into the Rural Housing Service (community facilities, technical assistance, and outreach), Rural Business-Cooperative Service (cooperatives, Business and Industry loans) and the Rural Utilities Service (electric, telecommunications, water).[6] The legislation also abolished the Rural Electrification Administration established under the Rural Electrification Act of 1936 establishing the Rural Utilities Service as its successor.

Federal Agriculture Improvement and Reform Act of 1996 (P.L. 104-127)

(The 1996 omnibus farm bill.) Title VII was the Rural Development title. Several major initiatives were established in this legislation including the following:

- Revised the rural distance learning and medical link programs into programs to finance the construction of facilities and systems to provide rural areas with telemedicine and distance learning services.
- Amended the Consolidated Farm and Rural Development Act to increase the amount of grants authorized to be made by the Secretary for water and waste facilities. Revised the definition of "rural" and "rural area," for the purposes of eligibility for grants and loans for such facilities, to limit eligibility to only those cities, towns, or unincorporated areas with populations of no more than 10,000.
- Established mandatory funding for a Fund for Rural America for rural research, economic development, and housing.
- Established the Rural Community Advancement Program (RCAP), a consolidated program of grants, loans, guarantees, and other assistance to local communities and federally recognized Indian tribes.

Farm Security and Rural Investment Act of 2002 (P.L. 107-171)

This legislation, enacted in May 2002, is the most recent omnibus farm bill. Title VI, in addition to providing funds for various rural loan and grant programs, also authorizes several new rural development initiatives. Major new initiatives include provisions funded through direct (mandatory) spending. Mandatory programs do not require annual appropriations. Funding is made available either through the Treasury or from the Commodity Credit Corporation. For FY2002-2007, new mandatory programs include:

- The Rural Strategic Investment Fund establishes a National Board on Rural America that will provide $100 million in planning grants to certified Regional Investment Boards.

- The Rural Business Investment Program provides $100 million in loan guarantees and subsidies to form Rural Business Investment corporations that will make equity investments to small firms. The program will be administered through the Small Business Administration.
- Enhanced Access to Broadband Service to Rural Areas provides $10-$20 million per year, FY2002-2007, in grants and loans.
- Rural Local Television Broadcast Signal Loan Guarantees authorizes $80 million under the Launching Our Communities' Access to Local Television Act of 2000.
- Value-added Agricultural Product Market Development Grants provide $40 million per year, FY2002-2007, to independent producers and producer-owned enterprises. There is also a 5% set-aside for organic production. $15 million of this funding is earmarked for 10 new Agriculture Innovation Centers for technical assistance to value-added agricultural businesses. The 10 centers were named in FY2003.
- The Rural America Infrastructure Development Account authorizes a one-time funding of pending water and waste water applications at $360 million;
- Rural Firefighters and Emergency Personnel Grant Program provides $10 million per year, FY2003-2007 funding to train emergency personnel.

The legislation also repealed the Fund for Rural America established in the 1996 farm bill.

USDA MISSION AGENCIES

The following sections outline the various loan and grant programs administered by the three principal USDA Rural Development mission agencies: Rural Housing Service (RHS), Rural Business-Cooperative Service (RBS), and Rural Utilities Service (RUS). Program objectives, statutory authority, eligibility, and FY2003-2004 and FY2005 (Administration requested) funding levels are provided. An overview of the Rural Community Advancement Program (RCAP) and the Office of Community Development is also provided.

USDA RURAL HOUSING SERVICE (RHS)

Rural Housing Issues: Background [7]

Key characteristics of rural housing needs are suggested by the following:

- Rural areas have a disproportionate share of the nation's substandard housing;
- There is a high incidence of poverty in rural America;
- There is an inadequate supply of affordable rural housing to meet demand;
- Mobile homes are increasingly pervasive in rural areas;
- Homeownership is the principal form of housing in rural America;
- Rural households pay more of their income for housing than their urban counterparts;
- Hundreds of rural communities nationwide do not have access to clean drinking water and safe waste disposal systems;
- Development costs in rural areas are often disproportionately higher;
- Rural residents may have more limited access to mortgage credit;
- Rural minorities are less likely to own their homes than rural white households.[8]

Housing Act of 1949 (P.L. 81-171) (42 U.S.C. 1441 Et Seq)

The preamble to this landmark legislation declares that every American deserves a "decent home and a suitable living environment." Housing in the post-World War II era was in short supply and many cities had housing that was in deteriorating condition. The Housing Act for the first time placed the federal government in the role of physically shaping U.S. urban and suburban areas. In doing so, the act influenced state and local polices regarding not only housing, but more broadly, social welfare policy, race relations, and economic development decisions. The act was significant in its creation of a new federal role, but it also was significant in establishing housing as a central policy focus, a focus that is more diminished today.

To meet the goals of more and better housing, Title I of the Housing Act financed slum clearance under urban redevelopment/renewal programs. Title

II increased authorization for Federal Housing Administration mortgage insurance. Title III committed the federal government to building 810,000 new public housing units by 1955.[9] While the provisions of these titles were strongly influenced by cities and their immediately adjacent suburban areas, the Housing Act also particularly recognized the shortages and low-quality housing that characterized much of rural America.

Title V of the act gave authorization to the Farmers Home Administration to grant mortgages for the purchase or repair of rural single-family houses. Title V authorized financial assistance in rural areas to farmers, owners, developers, and elderly persons for the purchase of rural property and construction of adequate facilities, insurance on various loans, and financial assistance for low rent housing for farm workers. Through the Rural Housing Insurance Fund Program account established by the Housing and Urban Development Act of 1965 (P.L. 89-117), the USDA Rural Housing Service today, as with the Farmers Home Administration in the past, insures and guarantees a variety of housing loans.

The Housing and Urban Development Act of 1968 (P.L. 90-448) (42 U.S.C. 1441a) (82 Stat. 476)

This legislation reaffirmed the 1949 Housing Act, but also placed greater emphasis on the failures of the 1949 Act to address the problems of housing for low-income families. The 1968 Act authorized the Federal Housing Administration's Section 235 homeownership program with the goal of expanding homeownership, especially among low-income families. The 1968 Act had the goal of creating nearly 26 million new units of housing, 6 million of which were to be reserved for low-income persons. The legislation enacts the New Communities Act of 1968, National Flood Insurance Act of 1968, Urban Property Protection and Reinsurance Act of 1968, and Interstate Land Sales Full Disclosure Act. The 1968 Act also created the Government National Mortgage Association (Ginnie Mae).

Rural Housing Amendments of 1983 (P.L. 98-181) (42 U.S.C. 1490k to 1490o)

Titles I through V are also referred to as the Housing and Urban-Rural Recovery Act of 1983. It amends the Housing and Community Development Act of 1974 and the United States Housing Act of 1937. Title V amends the

1949 Housing Act to require that at least 40% of all dwelling units financed by a rural housing loan through the Farmers Home Administration and at least 30% of such units in each state be available only for very low-income persons and families. It authorizes loans for manufactured homes and lots meeting specified safety standards and installation, structural, site and energy conserving requirements, whether such homes and lots are real property, personal property, or both.

Housing Legislation in the 108th Congress

Rural rental housing and affordable housing are important housing concerns in the 108th Congress. Several bills addressing these and other housing issues included:

- **H.R. 839.** Renewing the Dream Tax Credit Act. Amends the Internal Revenue Code of 1986 to provide rural rental housing assistance. The bill gives priority to very low-income families, low-income communities, communities lacking affordable rental housing, or certain other applicants.
- **S. 1248/H.R. 1102.** National Affordable Housing Trust Fund Act of 2003. This legislation provides funds to build, restore and preserve 1.5 million affordable housing units for very low-income households over the next 10 years. Modeled on the more than 280 state and local housing trust funds, the Trust Fund is intended to help families earning less than 30 percent of the local median income.
- **H.R. 1722.** Rural Rental Housing Act of 2003. This bill authorizes the Secretary of Agriculture to provide rural rental assistance, with applicant priority given to very low income families, low-income communities, rural areas, and communities with severe lack of affordable rental housing. Eligible rural areas are those with 25,000 or less population.
- **H.R. 1088/S. 532.** Colonias Gateway Initiative Act. Authorizes the Secretary of Housing and Urban Development to make grants
- through September 30, 2009, to regional organizations to enhance the availability of affordable housing, economic opportunity, and infrastructure in the colonias. Colonias are recognized communities along the United States-Mexico border region in Arizona, California, New Mexico, and Texas. These communities lack such

services as potable water, adequate sewage systems, and safe and sanitary housing.

- **H.R. 2740.** Rural Multifamily Housing Loan Guarantee and Ginnie Mae Corrections Act. The bill amends the National Housing Act of 1949 to authorize the Government National Mortgage Association (Ginnie Mae) to guarantee securities backed by loans insured or guaranteed by the Rural Housing Service under Title V of the Housing Act of 1949.
- **H.R. 3485.** Affordable Housing Preservation Tax Relief Act of 2003. This legislation would amend the Internal Revenue Code of 1986 to provide a tax incentive to preserve affordable housing in multifamily housing units which are sold or exchanged.
- **S. 1205.** Rural Teacher Housing Act of 2003. The bill requires the Secretary of Housing and Urban Development to provide grants to states with a population of fewer than 1 million people and to make grants to eligible school districts located within a population of 6,500 or fewer. The grants may be used for (1) construction of new housing units within a qualified municipality; (2) the purchase and rehabilitation of existing housing units within a qualified municipality; or (3) the rehabilitation of housing units within a qualified municipality that are owned by an eligible school district.
- **H.R. 284/S. 595.** Housing Bond and Credit Modernization and Fairness Act of 2003. Legislation would amend the Internal Revenue Code of 1986 to modify the housing purchase price limitation under mortgage subsidy bond rules based on median family income.

Rural Housing Service Programs

The following programs are authorized by the Housing Act of 1949 and include programs for individual homeownership and rental housing. They, accordingly, do not require annual reauthorization or reauthorization in periodic omnibus farm bills. Budget authorization is expressed in terms of loan *subsidies* and loan *authority*. Housing loan subsidies are transfers from the Treasury to lenders who may then provide loans at reduced interest rates to low-income borrowers who otherwise would not be able to obtain credit under a lender's usual criteria. Loan authority refers to the total value of all loans made under a particular program. A subsidy "leverages" a larger loan amount. A small total loan subsidy permits a relatively large amount of principal actually lent. Loan authorization refers to the total amount of loan indebtedness that a particular program may assume.

Funding for Rural Housing Service homeownership programs is provided by the Rural Housing Insurance Fund through three financing mechanisms: (1) direct loans, (2) guaranteed loans, and (3) grants. Direct loans are loans whose principal is subsidized by the federal government. The principal for a guaranteed loan is provided by a private lender, but the lender is protected by the federal government in the event a borrower defaults. If a guaranteed loan is made at market interest rates and the default rate is zero, then the cost to the federal government for making the guaranteed loan is zero. A grant is a direct outlay to an applicant, often on the basis of a competition for funds. Funding limits for individual grants and total levels of loan authorization are stated in legislation authorizing the loans and grants.

Section 502 Single Family Housing Direct Loan Program

This is USDA's main housing loan program and is designed to help low-income individuals purchase houses in rural areas. Funds can also be used to build, repair, or renovate a house, including providing water and sewage facilities. The program provides fixed-interest mortgage financing to low-income families who are unable to obtain credit elsewhere. The program also provides "supervised credit" including pre-loan and post-loan credit counseling to its borrowers to help them maintain their homes during financial crises. While the program benefits rural areas nationwide, the highest benefits (in per capita dollars) were in low-income areas such as the Delta South and rapidly growing areas in the West.

Statutory Authority: Title V, Section 502 of the Housing Act of 1949; 42 U.S.C., Chapter 8A, Subchapter III, 1471, et seq.

Financing: Loans are subsidized at a graduated interest rate from 1% over Treasury's cost of money, depending on family income. Applicants may obtain 100% financing and loans are for up to 33 years (38 years for those with incomes below 60% of the area median household income). Interest rates are determined so that a family pays from 22% to 26% of their income for principal, interest, taxes, and insurance.

Eligibility: Borrowers must be either very-low income (less than 50% of median family income in the rural area where they reside) or low-income (50-80% of median family income). Housing must be modest in size, design, and cost.[10]

Funding: Total loan authorization in FY2003: $1.04 billion; FY2004: $1.35 billion; FY2005: $1.100 billion (est.). Lend subsidies (budget authority) FY2003: $201.0 million; FY2004: $125.3 million; FY2005: $127.4 million (est).

Section 502 Guaranteed Single Family Housing Purchase and Refinance Loans

Provides loan guarantees to private lenders for low and moderate income families to purchase housing. Objective is to provide an incentive to private lenders to offer loans for 30-year mortgages to rural residents who would otherwise be unable to obtain credit.

> **Statutory Authority:** Title V, Section 502 of the Housing Act of 1949; 42 U.S.C., Chapter 8A, Subchapter III, 1471, et seq.
> **Financing:** The government guarantees 90% of loan principal as an encouragement to private lenders to make loans to rural residents whose incomes are between 80 and 115% of the median county income. Loans may be up to 100% of market value or acquisition costs, whichever is less. There is no down payment requirement.
> **Funding:** Loan authorization in FY2003: $3.09 billion; FY2004: $2.71 billion; FY2005 (est.): $2.73 billion. Loan subsidies (budget authority) in FY2003: $35.2 million; FY2004: $39.7 million; FY2005: $33.7 million (est.).

Section 504 Very Low-Income Rural Housing and Repair Loan and Grant Program

This program provides loan and grant assistance to very-low and low-income homeowners to make housing repairs that remove various health and safety hazards from their houses or to improve or modernize a home.

> **Statutory Authority:** Title V, Section 504 of the Housing Act of 1949; 42 U.S.C., Chapter 8A, Subchapter III, 1471, et seq.
> **Financing:** Loans of up to $20,000 and grants of up to $7,500 are available.
> **Eligibility Criteria:** Loans are available to very low-income rural residents who own and occupy a dwelling in need of repair. A homeowner must be unable to obtain affordable credit elsewhere. Grants are limited to elderly home owners (age 62 and older) whose incomes are 50% or less of the median in the rural area where they reside. Grant funds may be used only for removal of a health or safety hazard.
> **Funding:** Loan authorization in FY2003: $31.6 million; FY2004: $34.8 million; FY2005(est): $35 million. Loan subsidies (budget authority) in FY2003: $9.8 million; FY2004: $9.6 million; FY2005 (est.): $10.2 million. Grants in FY2003: $31.5 million; FY2004: $30.1 million; FY2005: $31.5 million.

Section 514 and 516 Farm Labor Housing Program Loan and Grant Program

This is the only nationwide program to provide housing for farm laborers.[11] Loans and grants are provided to buy, build, improve, or repair housing for farm labor, including persons whose income is earned in aquaculture and on-farm processing. Section 516 grants are used in conjunction with the loans to finance affordable, off-farm rental housing to low-wage farm workers

> **Statutory Authority:** Title V, Section 514 and 516 of the Housing Act of 1949; 42 U.S.C., Chapter 8A, Subchapter III, 1484 and 1486.
>
> **Financing:** This program provides direct loans to farm owners, Indian tribes, farmer associations, public bodies, and nonprofit organizations to provide living quarters, furnishings, and related facilities for domestic farm workers. Section 514 loans have a 1% interest rate and a maximum repayment term of 33 years. Grants may cover up to 90% of development costs.
>
> **Eligibility Criteria:** Farmworkers who lease Section 514/516 units must be either U.S. citizens or permanent residents and the majority of their income must come from farm work. Grants are available only to governments or nonprofit organizations.
>
> **Funding:** Loan authorization in FY2003: $55.9 million ($27.4 million in subsidies) and $5.8 million in grants; FY2004: $42.6 million ($18.2 in loan subsidies) and $17.9 million in grants; FY2005 (est.): $36.7 million ($19.8 in loan subsidies) $17 million in grants.

Section 523 Mutual Self-Help Grant Program

This program allows very-low and low income rural Americans to use "sweat equity" to reduce the costs of home ownership. Nonprofit organizations and local governments may obtain grant funds to enable them to provide technical assistance to groups of families that work cooperatively to build their houses. Typically, future homeowners use Section 502 direct loans to finance their mortgages and, through their own labor on constructing the house are able to reduce costs by 10-15% while learning construction skills.

> **Statutory Authority:** Title V, Section 523 (b)(1)(A) of the Housing Act of 1949; 42 U.S.C. 1490(c)(B).
>
> **Financing:** Grants. Grantees typically also use Section 502 loans although other mortgage tools are also used. Funds may be used to pay salaries, rent, and office expenses of the participating nonprofit organizations. Pre-development grants up to $10,000 are available to qualified organizations.

Eligibility Criteria: Low income (50%-80% of area median family income)
Funding: Grants for FY2003: $40.1 million; FY2004: $33.8 million; FY2005: $34.0 million (est.).

Section 523 Rural Housing Site Loan Program

This program provides funds to nonprofit organizations to develop building sites for low and moderate-income participants in the Self-Help Housing Program. The nonprofit organizations resell these improved sites to program participants at cost. The interest rate on the loans is 3% and the nonprofit organizations repay the loans when they sell these properties.

Statutory Authority: Title V, Section 523 (b)(1)(A) of the Housing Act of 1949; 42 U.S.C. 1490(c)(B).
Financing: Loans are for two years. Section 523 loans bear 3% interest rates.
Eligibility Criteria: Section 523 loans are made to acquire and develop sites only for housing constructed by the self-help method.
Funding: Loan authorization FY2003: $978,000 million; FY2004: $2.4 million; FY2005 (est.): $5.0 million. Subsidy levels (budget authority) FY2003: $220,000; FY2004: $75,000; FY2005: $0 (est.).

Section 524 Rural Housing Site Loan Program

This program is very similar to the Section 523 program above except that once the sites are developed, they may be provided to any low- or moderate-income person, not just to the self-help participant.

Statutory Authority: Title V, Section 524 (b)(1)(A) of the Housing Act of 1949; 42 U.S.C. 1480(d).
Financing: Loans are for two years. Section 524 loans bear the market rate of interest.
Eligibility Criteria: Section 524 loans are made to acquire and develop sites for any low-or moderate-income family.
Funding: Loan authorization in FY2003: $5.0 million; FY2004: $5.0 million; FY2005 (est.): $5.0 million. Loan subsidies (budget authority) in FY2003: $55,000; FY2004: $0; FY2005 (est.): $0.

Section 533 Housing Preservation Grant Program

This program provides funding through nonprofit groups, Indian tribes, and government agencies to very-low and low-income home owners to repair their houses, and to rental property owners for the rehabilitation of rental and cooperative housing to be rented to very-low and low-income families.

Statutory Authority: Title V, Section 533 of the Housing Act of 1949; 42 U.S.C., Chapter 8A, Subchapter III, 1480m.
Financing: Grants.
Eligibility Criteria: Low and very-low income rural residents. Grants may also be made to rental property owners if they agree to make such units available to low and very-low income occupants.
Funding: For FY2003: $10.1 million; FY2004: $9.9 million; FY2005 (est.): $10.0 million.

Section 515 Rural Rental Housing Direct Loans

The Section 515 rental housing program houses the poor through 50-year, 1% loans and rental assistance. The program is typically used in conjunction with the Section 521 Rental Assistance Program (see below). With assistance, tenants pay a maximum of 30% of their income toward rent and utilities. Some 515 projects also use Housing and Urban Development Section 8 project-based assistance which enables additional very-low income families to be helped. There are four variations of the Section 515 loan program: (1) Cooperative Housing, (2) Downtown Renewal Areas, (3) Congregate Housing or Group Homes for Persons with Disabilities, and (4) the Rural Housing Demonstration Program.

Statutory Authority: Title V, Section 515 of the Housing Act of 1949; 42 U.S.C. 1490(c).
Financing: This program uses a public-private partnership to provide direct subsidized interest loans at 1% interest rate to limited-profit and nonprofit developers to construct or to renovate affordable rental complexes in rural areas.
Eligibility Criteria: For very-low, low-, and moderate-income families. In new Section 515 projects, 95% of tenants must have very-low incomes. In existing projects 75% of new tenants must have very low incomes.
Funding: Loan authorization for FY2003: $115.1 million; FY2004: $115.9 million; FY2005 (est.): $60.0 million. Loan subsidies (budget authority) for FY2003: $53.6 million; FY2004: $49.8 million; FY2005 (est.): $28.3 million.

Section 538 Multi-Family Guaranteed Loan Program

The program funds construction, acquisition, and rehabilitation of multifamily housing for low to moderate-income residents. It provides 90% loan guarantees to certified lenders to make rental housing affordable to low and moderate-income residents. For the nonprofit sector, the program covers 97% loan-to-value ratios.

Statutory Authority: Title V, Section 538 of the Housing Act of 1949; 42 U.S.C. 1485.

Financing: Guarantees market-rate loans made by private lenders.

Eligibility Criteria: Residents of the completed housing facility must be very low- to moderate-income households; or elderly, or disabled persons with income not in excess of 115% of the median income of the surrounding area.

Funding: Loan authorization in FY2003: $99.1 million; FY2004: $99.4 million; FY2005 (est.): $100 million. Loan subsides (budget authority) for FY2003: $4.5 million; FY2004: $5.9 million; FY2005 (est.): $3.5 million.

Section 521 Rental Assistance Program

The objective of this program is to help mitigate the burden on the nearly 25% of rural households who pay more than 30% of their income on housing costs.

Statutory Authority: Title V, Section 521(a)(2) of the Housing Act of 1949; 42 U.S.C. 1490.

Financing: Rental Assistance is project-based assistance used in conjunction with Section 515 and Section 514/516 loan/grant programs. The program provides rental assistance directly to the owners of some RHS-financed projects under contracts specifying that beneficiaries will pay no more than 30% of their income for rent. The program makes up the difference between the tenant's contribution and the rental charge.

Eligibility Criteria: The subsidy goes to the housing unit, not an individual tenant. In effect, the subsidy indirectly goes to the tenant through lower rent payments.

Funding: FY2003: $721.1 million; FY2004: $574.1 million; FY2005 (est.): $586.0 million.

Housing Demonstration Program

Under this program, RHS may provide loans to low income borrowers to purchase innovative housing units and systems that do not meet existing published standards, rules, regulations, or policies. The objective of the demonstration programs is to test new approaches to constructing housing under the statutory authority granted to the Secretary of Agriculture. The intended effect is to increase the availability of affordable rural housing for low-income families through innovative designs and systems.

Statutory Authority: Title V, Section 506(b), Housing Act of 1949; 42 U.S.C. 1476.

Financing: Loans and grants. Aggregate expenditures for the demonstration may not exceed $10 million in any fiscal year.

Eligibility Criteria: Section 506 (b) requires that the health and safety of the population of the areas in which the demonstrations are carried out will not be adversely affected.

Funding: Program funding is reserved through other RHS programs listed above. In FY2004, $5 million is provided for a demonstration housing program for processing workers in Alaska, Mississippi, Utah, and Wisconsin.

USDA RURAL BUSINESS-COOPERATIVE SERVICE (RBS)

Creating and retaining employment in rural areas has been a central focus of rural development policies for nearly 75 years. Originally, agriculture, mining, fishing, and timbering related jobs were major targets of public funding. Since the mid-1950s, manufacturing was regarded as the most promising source of rural employment as jobs in the primary sector declined. Abundant and largely non-unionized labor, inexpensive land, and minimal environmental regulation were rural America's competitive advantage as many manufacturing facilities sought branch production facilities. While manufacturing has provided relatively high-paying and stable employment for many rural residents, the U.S. rural manufacturing sector finds itself today competing with developing countries and with Eastern Europe. Low-skilled, peripheral manufacturing facilities are leaving U.S. rural areas. Today, rural areas are trying to create new sources of competitive advantage in more technologically sophisticated production with higher-skill labor. With lack of capital a significant factor in many rural areas, the RBS provides loans and grants to help local entrepreneurs in starting up businesses and in expanding existing businesses.[12] Other RBS programs provide specialized technical and marketing assistance. Several programs authorized in the 2002 farm bill (P.L.107-171) address the new needs of rural businesses, especially in capital formation.

Rural Intermediary Relending Program

These direct loans are made to private nonprofit corporations, state or local government agencies, Indian tribes, and cooperatives who, in turn, lend the funds to rural businesses, private nonprofit organizations, and others. Assistance from the intermediary to the ultimate recipient must be for economic development projects, establishment of new businesses, and/or expansion of existing businesses, creation of new employment opportunities and/or saving existing rural jobs.

Statutory Authority: Health and Human Services Act of 1986, Section 407, P.L. 99-425, 7 U.S.C. 1932 note; Food Security Act of 1985, Section 1323, as amended, P.L.99-198, 7 U.S.C. 1631; Community Economic Development Act of 1981, Section 623, as amended, P.L.97-35, 42 U.S.C. 9812. ;7 U.S.C. 1932; 42 U.S.C. 9812.
Financing: Loans are made by RBS to intermediaries that provide loans to ultimate recipients for business facilities and community development projects.
Criteria: Financing is limited to community development projects not within the outer boundary of any city having a population of 25,000 or more.
Funding: Loan authorization for FY2003: $39.7 million; FY2004: $39.8 million; FY2005:$34.2 million (est.). Loan subsidies (budget authority) for FY2003: $19.2 million; FY2004: $17.2 million; FY2005 (est.): $15.9 million.

Rural Economic Development Loans

This program provides zero-interest loans for RUS borrowers who then re-lend the funds at zero interest to rural businesses.

Statutory Authority: Rural Electrification Act of 1936, as amended, Title III, 7 U.S.C. 930-940c; 7 U.S.C. 1932(a).
Financing: Direct loans.
Eligibility Criteria: Loans are made to electric and telephone utilities that have current loans with the Rural Utilities Service (RUS) or Rural Telephone Bank loans or guarantees outstanding and are not delinquent on any federal debt or in bankruptcy proceedings.
Funding: Loan authorization for FY2003: $14.9 million; FY2004: $14.9 million; FY2005 (est.): $25.0 million. Loan subsidies (budget authority) for FY2003: $3.2 million; FY2004: $2.8 million; FY2005 (est.): $4.7 million.

Rural Economic Development Grants

Grants are used to establish a revolving loan fund program to promote economic development in rural areas. The revolving loan fund provides capital to nonprofit organizations and municipal organizations to finance community facilities in rural areas that promote job creation and education and training to enhance marketable skills, or improve medical care.

Statutory Authority: Section 313 of the Rural Electrification Act of 1936; 7 U.S.C. 930-940(c); 7 U.S.C. 1932.
Financing: Grants. Funds are provided from the interest differential on Rural Utilities Service borrowers' cushion of credit accounts. The cushion of credit account was established under Section 313 of the Rural Electrification Act (REA). Under this program, RUS borrowers may make voluntary deposits into a special cushion of credit account. A borrower's cushion of credit account balance accrues interest to the borrower at an annual rate of 5%. The amounts in the cushion of credit account (deposits and earned interest) can only be used to make scheduled payments on loans made or guaranteed under REA.
Eligibility Criteria: Economic development projects benefitting rural areas. Funding may be used for feasibility studies, start-up costs, and incubator projects.
Funding: FY2003: $4.1 million; FY2004: $4.0 million; FY2005 (est.): $4.0 million.

Rural Cooperative Development Grants

The grants were established under the 1996 farm bill (P.L. 104-127) which eliminated the term "technology " from the previously authorized Rural Technology and Cooperative Development Grant Program. Grants are made to fund the establishment and operation of centers for rural cooperative development with their primary purpose being the improvement of economic conditions in rural areas through the creation of new or improvement of cooperatives. Grants may be made to nonprofit institutions or higher education institutions. Grants may be used to pay up to 75% of the cost of the project and associated administrative costs. The applicant must contribute 25% from non-federal sources. Grants under this program are competitive and awarded on specific selection criteria.

Statutory Authority: Section 310 B(e) of the Consolidated Farm and Rural Development Act of 1972; 7 U.S.C. 1932(e); 42 U.S.C. 9817.

Financing: Grants.
Eligibility Criteria: Grants to nonprofit corporations and institutions of higher education. For this program, rural is defined as all territories of a state not within the outer boundary of any city having a population of 50,000 or more based on the latest decennial census of the United States.
Funding: FY2003: $5.4 million; FY2004: $5.0 million; FY2005: $3.5 million (est.).

Appropriate Technology Transfer for Rural Areas (ATTRA) Program

A cooperative agreement established by the 1985 farm bill, the program was transferred to the Department of Interior's Fish and Wildlife Service in 1990. The 1996 farm bill transferred the program back to USDA's Rural Business Service. The program is an account of the Rural Cooperative Grants program. It provides information to farmers and other rural users on a variety of sustainable agricultural practices that include both cropping and livestock operations. The ATTRA program is located on the University of Arkansas campus at Fayetteville, Arkansas, and functions as an information and technical assistance center staffed with sustainable agriculture specialists.

Statutory Authority: Section 1323 of the Food Security Act of 1985; 7 U.S.C. 1932.
Financing: The program is funded through a cooperative agreement between the not-for-profit National Center for Appropriate Technology and the Rural Business-Cooperative Service.
Eligibility Criteria: Open.
Funding: For FY2003: $2.5 million; FY2004: $2.5 million; FY2005: $0.

Value-Added Agricultural Production Market Development Grants

The program provides grants to assist farmers and ranchers in creating greater value for agricultural commodities. A provision in the 2002 farm bill makes mandatory funding for this program to FY2007. A portion of the fund was reserved for the establishment of Agricultural Demonstration Centers which will provide training and technical assistance to new or expanding value-added agricultural enterprises. Ten centers were established in FY2003 and funded at $1 million each.

> **Statutory Authority:** Agricultural Risk Protection Act of 2000 (P.L.106-224); Section 6401 of the Farm Security and Rural Investment Act of 2002 (P.L.107-171).
> **Financing:** Competitive grants.
> **Eligibility Criteria:** Profit and nonprofit organizations, cooperatives.
> **Funding:** FY2003: $19.8 million;[13] FY2004: $14.9 million; FY2005: $15.5 million (est.).

National Sheep Industry Improvement Center

Established by the 1996 farm bill, this program is an industry-driven education and marketing program directed at enhancing the U.S. sheep and goat industry. The program provides seed-money that promotes investment to allow the program to become independent by 2006.

> **Statutory Authority:** Federal Agricultural Improvement and Reform Act of 1996; 7 U.S.C. 2008j.
> **Financing:** A revolving fund providing a variety of financing mechanisms, e.g., direct and guaranteed loans, grants.
> **Eligibility Criteria:** Eligible entities include public, private, or cooperative organizations, associations, including corporations not operated for profit, Federally recognized Indian tribes, or public or quasi-public agencies. An individual is not considered an eligible entity. Fifty-one percent of the entity must be owned by citizens of the United States or reside in the United States after being legally admitted for permanent residence.
> **Funding:** Initially, $20 million was authorized to establish the fund, without fiscal year limitations. Additional appropriations for FY2003: $850,000 FY2004: $496,000; FY2005 (est.): $0. The center is scheduled to be privatized by April 2006.

Rural Business Investment Program

This program was established by the 2002 Farm Bill and creates limited liability companies (Rural Business Investment Companies) to make equity capital investments in rural businesses. These companies will be financed with both private funds and debt instruments guaranteed by the federal government. The program will be operated under a Memorandum of

Agreement with the U.S. Department of Commerce's Small Business Administration.

> **Statutory Authority:** Section 6029, Farm Security and Rural Investment Act of 2002 (P.L. 107-171).
> **Financing:** Direct loans, guaranteed debentures, and grants.
> **Eligibility Criteria:** Designation by the Secretary as a Rural Business Company.
> **Funding:** "Such sums as necessary" are authorized to cover the costs of guaranteeing a total of $280 million of debentures. In addition, $44 million in mandatory funding is authorized for grants and $56 million for direct loan subsidies. A portion of the mandatory funding for the program was blocked by appropriators in FY2003 and FY2004 while providing some initial funding to begin the program. Additional grant funding is requested for FY2005, while cancelling the remaining portion of the authorization. For FY2005, the Administration has also requested a reduction in the level of debentures.

Rural Strategic Investment Program

This program was established by the 2002 farm bill. It establishes a National Board on Rural America that will make planning grants and innovations grants to certified Regional Investment Boards. As with the Rural Business Investment Program above, this program is also designed to address the general lack of investment capital in many rural areas.

> **Statutory Authority:** Section 6030, Farm Security and Rural Investment Act of 2002 (P.L. 107-171).
> **Financing:** Planning grants and innovation grants.
> **Eligibility Criteria:** Designation by the Secretary as a Regional Investment Board.
> **Funding:** The program was authorized for $100 million in mandatory funding in FY2002. Those funds were not distributed in FY2002 and the funding carried over to FY2003. Appropriators prohibited the expenditure of any funds to carry out the program in FY2003 and FY2004. The Administration requests that funds be cancelled for FY2005.

Renewable Energy Loan and Grant Program

This program provides funding to eligible farmers, ranchers, and small businesses in purchasing renewable energy systems and making existing energy systems more efficient.

Statutory Authority: Section 9006, Farm Security and Rural Investment Act of 2002 (P.L. 107-171).
Financing: Loans and grants.
Eligibility Criteria:
Funding: The program was authorized for $23 million in mandatory funds per fiscal year, FY2003-FY2007. Appropriators prohibited the expenditure of any of the mandatory funds to carry out the program in FY2003 and FY2004, but did provide $22.8 million in discretionary funding for the program in FY2004. The Administration has requested cancelling the mandatory funding for FY2005 and providing $10.7 million in discretionary funding.

USDA RURAL UTILITIES SERVICE (RUS)

Arguably, the earliest rural development policy consisted of providing infrastructure to get rural products to markets or to transportation nodes. Building railroads and telegraph lines represented early examples. Later electricity and telephones constituted essential rural infrastructure. Because of great geographical distances and low population densities, rural areas would unlikely have had such services without federal support. The 1936 Rural Electrification Act discussed above was central to the provision of rural utilities in an urbanizing society. Today, rural electrification, telecommunications, and water infrastructure are the core programs administered by the Rural Utilities Service.[14] New infrastructure includes facilities for health service delivery, e.g., telemedicine, and new broadband telecommunication resources. As in the early years of the Nation, great distances and sparse populations have also led Congress to provide funding for these new rural utilities as well as continuing support for telephones and electrical generation and transmission.

Electric Loan Program

Loans are made to expand, upgrade, maintain, and replace rural electric infrastructure. Interest rates are tied to the economic conditions of the areas served and the costs of providing services to the area. Most RUS-financed systems have their loan rates capped at 7% although there are three interest rate levels: (1) direct loans for distressed areas, (2) Treasury rate loans, and (3) municipal rate loans. Borrowers must generally obtain approximately half their capital needs from the private sector. RUS also makes guaranteed loans through the Federal Financing Bank, National Bank for Cooperatives, and National Rural Utilities Cooperative Finance Cooperation. The interest rate on loans by the Federal Financing Bank is based on the Treasury rate plus 1/8%. Because of a very low default rate, the FFB loan guarantee program has a zero subsidy cost. Most loans are made for 35 years and are secured by the borrower's electric system assets.

> **Statutory Authority:** Section 305, Rural Electrification Act of 1936; 7 U.S.C. 904, 935.
> **Financing:** Three loan levels: Hardship loans are made to applicants whose consumers fall below average per capita and household income thresholds. Municipal rate loans are based on interest rates available in the municipal bond market. Borrowers are required to seek supplemental financing for 30% of their capital requirements. Treasury rate loans are based on rates established daily by the U.S. Treasury.
> **Eligibility Criteria:** Electricity producers and transmitters serving rural populations.
> **Funding:** Loan authorization levels for FY2003: $3.99 billion; FY2004: $4.99 billion; FY2005 (est.): $2.64 billion. Subsidies (budget authority) for FY2003: $29.4 million; FY2004: $60,000; FY2005 (est.): $5.1 million.[15]

Telecommunications Loans

This program makes loans for infrastructure improvement and expansion to furnish and improve telephone service, including a variety of related telecommunications purposes such as broadband service in rural areas. RUS lends directly to rural telecommunication systems and guarantees loans made by other lenders.

Statutory Authority: Rural Electrification Act of 1936; 7 U.S.C. 922.
Financing: Direct loans for construction, expansion, and operation of telecommunication lines and facilities or systems.
Eligibility Criteria: Three loan levels: Hardship loans are made to applicants whose consumers fall below average per capita and household income thresholds. Municipal rate loans are based on interest rates available in the municipal bond market. Treasury rate loans are based on rates established daily by the U.S. Treasury. Guaranteed loans are made through the Federal Financing Bank.
Funding: Telecommunication loan authorization levels for FY2003: $482.8 million; FY2004: $513.5 million; FY2005 (est.): $495.0 million. Loan subsidies (budget authority) for FY2003: $1.4 million; FY2004: $124,000; FY2005 (est.): $100,000.

Distance Learning and Telemedicine Loans and Grants

This program provides financial assistance to rural community facilities, e.g., schools, libraries, hospitals, and medical centers. The Telecommunications Act of 1996 targeted rural areas because of the difficulties they have in providing high quality education and medical services. This program helps rural schools and hospitals obtain and use advanced telecommunications for health and educational services.

Statutory Authority: Food, Agriculture, Conservation, and Trade Act of 1990; 7 U.S.C. 950 aaa-2 et seq.
Financing: Interest rates depend on the financial condition of the borrower system and the costs of providing service to rural subscribers. Cost of money loans are supplemented by loans from the Rural Telephone Bank. Most rural systems are eligible for loans at a hardship rate of 4%. The program also makes guaranteed loans.
Eligibility Criteria: Loans are made to utilities serving rural communities.
Funding: Grants and combination loan/grants ($10 in loans to $1 in grants). Loan authorization in FY2003: $20.7 million; FY2004: $300.0 million; FY2005: $0 (est.). Loan subsidies (budget authority) for FY2003: $0; FY2004: $0 million; FY2005: $0 (est.). Grant funding for FY2003: $33.5 million; FY2004: $24.8 million; FY2005: $25.0 million (est.).

Rural Telephone Bank

The Rural Telephone Bank (RTB) was designed to ensure rural telephone systems' access to private sources of capital by establishing a supplemental credit mechanism to which borrower systems may turn for all or part of their future capital requirements. The capital structure of the Telephone Bank consists of three classes of stock: Class A, Class B, and Class C. Class A stock was issued to the Telephone Bank in exchange for appropriated $600 million of capital provided by the taxpayers. This provided the Telephone Bank with its initial "seed" money to begin its lending operations. Through sales of Class A stock, the RTB is being privatized.

Statutory Authority: Rural Electrification Act of 1936; 7 U.S.C. 941, et seq.

Financing: Interest rates depend on the financial condition of the borrower system and the costs of providing service to rural subscribers. Most rural systems are eligible for loans at a hardship rate of 5%.

Eligibility Criteria: Utilities serving rural communities.

Funding: Loan authorization level FY2003: $167.8 million; FY2004: $173.5 million; FY2005 (est.): $0. Loan subsidies (budget authority) for FY2003: $2.3 million; FY2004: $0; FY2005: $0 (est.).

Broadband Loans and Grants

New telecommunication technologies will increasingly rely on infrastructure that can carry signals more complex than simple voice and at significantly faster speeds. Rural areas are currently at a disadvantage in gaining access to these newer technologies, in part, because the costs per user are higher than in more urbanized areas. RUS provides loans and grants to support acquisition./construction of broadband facilities in under-served rural areas.

Statutory Authority: Rural Electrification Act of 1936; 7 U.S.C. 922.

Financing: Interest rates on loans depend on the financial condition of the borrower system and the costs of providing service to rural subscribers. There are three interest rate levels: Three interest rate levels: hardship, Treasury, and municipal. Treasury loans may be supplemented by loans from the Rural Telephone Bank. Most rural systems are eligible for loans at a hardship rate of 4%.

Eligibility Criteria: The "community-oriented connectivity" approach will target rural, economically-challenged communities and offer a means for the deployment of broadband transmission services to rural schools, libraries, education centers, health care providers, law enforcement agencies, public safety organizations as well as residents and businesses. Community eligibility requirements for funding through the Community Connect Broadband Grant Program include areas with (1) 20,000 or fewer residents, (2) no prior access to a broadband transmission service; and (3) a minimum matching contribution equal to 15% of the grant amount awarded.

Funding: Loan authorization levels for FY2003: $0; FY2004: $598.1 million; FY2005 (est): $331.1 million. Loan subsidies (budget authority) for FY2003: $0; FY2004: $13.0 million; FY2005: $9.9 million. Broadband telecommunication grants for FY2003: $32.8 million; FY2004: $8.9 million; FY2005: $0 (est.).

Enhancement of Access to Broadband Service in Rural Areas

This program provides loans, grants, and loan guarantees to construct, improve, and acquire facilities and equipment to provide broadband service to rural areas with less than 20,000 residents.

Statutory Authority: Section 6103, Farm Security and Rural Investment Act of 2002 (P.L. 107-171).

Financing: Loans and grants. Loans are made at 4%.

Eligibility Criteria: Rural areas of less than 20,000 population and outside of an urban/metro commuting area.

Funding: Mandatory funding was authorized at $20 million per year, FY2002-2005 and $10 million in FY2006 and FY2007. Appropriators have blocked funding for the program in FY2002-2004. The Administration requests no funding for FY2005. Other RUS loan and grant programs provide discretionary funding for broadband (see above).

Local Television Loans

This program was authorized by the Launching Our Communities' Access to Local Television Act of 2000 (P.L. 106-553). The legislation provides for the establishment of the Local Television Loan Guarantee Board. The program facilitates access, on a technologically neutral basis, to signals of local television stations for households located in non-served or under-served areas.

Statutory Authority: Title X of the FY2001 Commerce, Justice, State Appropriations Act (P.L.106-553); 7 U.S.C. 1932(f).
Financing: Loan guarantees.
Eligibility Criteria: The Loan Guarantee Board is authorized to approve loan guarantees of up to 80% of the total loan amount for no more than $1.25 billion in loans.
Funding: Loan authorization level for FY2003: $0; FY2004: $0; FY2005: $0 (est.).

High Energy Cost Grants

The purpose of this grant program is to provide financial assistance for a broad range of energy facilities, equipment and related activities to offset the impacts of extremely high residential energy costs on eligible communities. Eligible facilities include on-grid and off-grid renewable energy systems and implementation of cost-effective demand side management and energy conservation programs that benefit eligible communities.

Statutory Authority: Rural Electrification Act of 1936; 7 U.S.C. 918(a).
Financing: Competitive grants. No cost sharing or matching funds are required as a condition of eligibility under this grant program. However, RUS will consider other financial resources available to the grantee and any voluntary commitment of matching funds or other contributions in assessing the grantee's capacity to carry out the grant program successfully and will award additional evaluation points to proposals that include such contributions. As a further condition of each grant, section 19(b)(2) of the RE Act requires that planning and administrative expenses may not exceed 4 percent of the grant funds.
Eligibility Criteria: Areas with high energy costs are those where the average residential expenditure for home energy is 275% of the national average.
Funding: For FY2003: $34.8; FY2004: $27.8 million; FY2005: $0.[16]

RURAL COMMUNITY ADVANCEMENT PROGRAM (RCAP)

The Rural Community Advancement Program (RCAP), one of the largest federal general assistance programs, was authorized by the 1996 farm bill, the Federal Agriculture Improvement and Reform Act (P.L. 104-127). The program consolidates funding for 12 rural development loan and grant programs into three accounts: Rural Community Facilities, Rural Utilities, and Rural Business-Cooperative Programs. RCAP was created as a mechanism to enhance the performance of many of USDA's categorical rural development programs. For example, the Community Facility Grant program reorganized by the 1996 farm bill is used in conjunction with existing loan and grant programs for the development of community facilities such as fire stations, community centers, and hospitals. RCAP also was designed to provide greater flexibility in targeting financial assistance to local needs by permitting a portion of the various accounts' funds to be shifted from one funding stream to another. Funding is allocated to state rural development offices where state directors set priorities on a state-by-state basis. State directors are authorized to transfer up to 25% of the amount in each RCAP account allocated for the state to any of the other accounts. Although RCAP has its own appropriation, the various programs consolidated under RCAP are administered by RHS, RBS, and RUS.

Within the three RCAP accounts discussed below, there are various funding earmarks for FY2003 and FY2004. The following table lists the FY2003-FY2004 funding for these earmarks and a brief description of the programs.

Earmark	Target	FY2003	FY2004
Federally Recognized Native American Tribes	Community facilities and economic development funding for Native American Tribes	$24 million	$24 million
Rural Community Development Initiative	See description below	$7 million	$6 million
Delta Regional Authority	Assistance to counties in the Mississippi Delta Region	$2 million	$1.75 million
Colonias	Water and waste water assistance to impoverished areas along the U.S.-Mexican border	$25 million	$25 million
Alaskan Villages	Community facilities and economic development in Alaska Native villages	$30 million	$28 million
Technical Assistance	For rural water and waste water systems	$18.3 million	$17.7 million
Circuit Rider Program	Technical assistance for rural water systems	$12.1 million	$13 million
Empowerment Zones/Enterprise Communities and Rural Economic Partnership Zones	See Section description below	$37.6 million	$22.1 million
Economic Impact Initiative Grants	Economic development funding for areas experiencing high unemployment and out-migration	$25 million	$22 million
High Energy Cost Grants	Funding for rural areas experiencing high residential energy costs	$30 million	$28 million
Tribal Colleges	Community facility grants for Native Tribal colleges	$4 million	$0
Rural Health Cooperatives	A demonstration program for home-based health care	$1 million	$0
Rural Community Assistance Program	Technical assistance to water and waste water systems	$5.5 million	$5.5 million

The following section provides an overview of the major components of RCAP's three accounts.

Community Facilities Account

Community Facility Direct and Guaranteed

Loans are made for constructing, enlarging, or improving essential community facilities in rural areas and towns of not more than 20,000 population. Eligible applicants must demonstrate that they cannot obtain funding in the commercial market at reasonable rates. Applications for health and public safety projects receive the highest priority. Interest rates are determined by the median family income of the area and range from 4.5% to 5.375%. In the case of guaranteed loans, the loans are made by a private lender and the interest rate is negotiated between lender and borrower.

Statutory Authority: Section 306(a)(1) of the Consolidated Agriculture and Rural Development Act of 1972.
Financing: Direct loan subsidies and guaranteed loans.
Eligibility Criteria: Priority is for loans to build essential community facilities that support public health and safety.
Funding: Loan authorization levels for *direct* loans in FY2003: $253.3 million; FY2004: $500.0 million; FY2005: $300.0 million (est). Subsidy levels for *direct* loans in FY2003: $15.8 million; FY2004: $0; FY2005: $12.2 million (est.). Loan authorization levels for *guaranteed* loans in FY2003: $161.2 million; FY2004: $210 million; FY2005: $210 million (est.).

Community Facility Grants

In most cases, these grants are used in conjunction with the direct loan program to make community facilities available, (e.g., fire stations, community centers) to the neediest communities, which often cannot afford even direct loans without additional subsidies. These grants were authorized under the 1996 farm bill (P.L.104-127).

Statutory Authority: Section 306(a)(1) of the Consolidated Agriculture and Rural Development Act of 1972.
Financing: Grants.
Eligibility Criteria: Low-income communities unable to secure funding on a loan basis. Public bodies, nonprofit organizations, special purpose districts, e.g., nursing homes, are eligible applicants. Funding is for communities of 20,000 or less. Priority is given to communities of 5,000 or less. Facility must serve areas where median household income is below the poverty line or 90%of the state non-metropolitan median household income.

Funding: FY2003: $18.5 million; FY2004: $15.8 million; FY2005: $17.0 million (est). Additional grant funds were earmarked in the Community
Facilities Account for Economic Impact Initiative Grants targeted to communities suffering economic hardship and population out-migration: FY2003: $23.3 million; FY2004: $21.9 million; FY2005: $0 million (est.).

Rural Community Development Initiative Grants

A new program authorized in FY2002. The program provides grants from RCAP accounts for capacity-building among private, nonprofit community development organizations and low-income rural communities in the areas of housing, community facilities, and community and economic development.

> **Statutory Authority:** Appropriation Act for Agriculture, Rural Development, Food and Drug Administration, P.L.106-387; 7 U.S.C. 1932.
> **Financing:** Competitive grants. Requires matching funds.
> **Eligibility Criteria:** Only qualified intermediary organizations are eligible for the technical assistance grants. Such organizations must supply matching funds from non-Federal sources to receive the grants.
> **Funding:** FY2003: $11.1 million; FY2004: $6.0 million; FY2005: $0 (est.).

Rural Business-Cooperative Account

Business and Industry (Bandi) Direct and Guaranteed Loans

This program finances business and industry acquisition, construction, conversion, expansion, and repair in rural areas. Loan funds can be used to finance the purchase and development of land, supplies and materials, and pay start-up costs of rural businesses. Eligible applicants include individuals as well as public, private, and cooperative organizations. Although the RBS did make direct loans to groups in FY2001 and in previous years, the FY2002 budget did not request direct funding due to a high rate of default.[17]

> **Statutory Authority:** Section 310B(a)(1) of the Consolidated Agriculture and Rural Development Act of 1972; 7 U.S.C. 1932.
> **Financing:** Subsidized interest loans and guarantees for loans provided by lenders. Interest rates for guaranteed loans are negotiated between a

lender and a borrower. A maximum guaranteed loan is $25 million. For loans of $5 million or less, maximum percentage of a guarantee is 80%. For loans between $5 and $10 million, maximum percentage of guarantee is 70%. For loans between $10 and $25 million, maximum percentage of guarantee is 60%.

Eligibility Criteria: Borrowers must be unable to obtain credit from other lenders at reasonable rates and terms. Criteria for projects are (1) those that save existing jobs, (2) improve existing businesses or industry and (3) create the greatest number of permanent jobs. Golf courses, race tracks, and gambling operations are ineligible.

Funding: Loan authorization level for *direct* loans in FY2003: $50.5 million with a loan subsidy of $2.9 million. No funding for the direct loan program was provided in FY2004 or requested for FY2005. Loan authorization levels for *guaranteed* loans in FY2003: $901.9 million with a loan subsidy of $35.8; million; FY2005: $600.0 million with a subsidy of $30.2 million (est.).

Rural Business Opportunity Grants

Grants are made to public bodies, nonprofit organizations, Indian tribes, and cooperatives for training and technical assistance to rural businesses, economic planning for rural communities, or training for rural entrepreneurs or economic development officials.

> **Statutory Authority:** Section 741, Federal Agriculture Improvement and Reform Act of 1996; Section 306(a)(11)(A) of the Consolidated Agriculture and Rural Development Act of 1972; 7 U.S.C. 1932.
> **Financing:** Competitive grants.
> **Eligibility Criteria:** Grants are made to public bodies, nonprofit corporations, Federally recognized tribal groups, and cooperatives with members that are primarily rural residents.
> **Funding:** FY2003: $3.1 million; FY2004: $3.0 million; FY2005: $3.0 million (est).

Rural Business Enterprise Grants

These are grants to encourage the development of small and emerging business enterprises; creation and expansion of rural distance learning networks; and to provide educational instruction or job training related to potential employment for adult students. Grants are also available to qualified nonprofit organizations for provision of technical assistance and training to rural communities for improving passenger transportation services or facilities.

Statutory Authority: Section 310N(c) and 310B(f) of the
Consolidated Agriculture and Rural Development Act of 1972; 7
U.S.C. 1932(c).
Financing: Competitive grants.
Eligibility Criteria: Priority for the grants is given to rural areas
having a population of 25,000 or less. Other priorities include projects
located in communities with large proportion of low-income residents
and/or high unemployment.
Funding: FY2003: $51.4 million; FY2004: $43.4 million; FY2005
(est.): $40.0 million (est.).

Rural Utilities Account

RCAP's Water and Waste loan and grant programs assist eligible
applicants in rural areas and cities and towns of up to 10,000 residents.
Drinking water, sanitary sewerage, solid waste disposal and storm drainage
facilities may be financed with direct and guaranteed loans and grants.
Applicants must be unable to finance their needs through their own resources
or with credit from commercial sources. The programs are administered by
state and local USDA Rural Development offices.

Water and Waste Disposal Direct and Guaranteed Loans

Loans are made to public bodies, organizations operated on a not-for-
profit basis, and Indian tribes on federal and state reservations for
development of storage, treatment, purification, or distribution of water or
for collection, treatment, and disposal of waste in rural areas. Loans are
repayable in not more than 40 years, or the useful life of the facility,
whichever is less.

Statutory Authority: Section 306 of the Consolidated Agriculture and
Rural Development Act of 1972; 7 U.S.C. 1926.
Financing: *Direct* loans carry interest rates not in excess of the current
market yield for comparable term municipal obligations. The interest
rate on loans cannot exceed 5% (they are currently being made at 4.5%)
for those areas where the (1) median household income of the service
area falls below the higher of 80% of the statewide non-metro median
household income or the poverty level; and (2) the project is needed to
meet applicable health or sanitary standards. The intermediate rate,
which is halfway between the poverty rate and the market rate, with a
ceiling of 7%, applies to those projects that do not meet the
requirements for the poverty rate but are located in areas where the
median household income does not exceed 100% of the statewide non-

metro median household income. *Guaranteed loans* are made to the same groups and for similar purposes except that loans are guaranteed by RUS for 80% of the loan amount or, in exceptional circumstances, 90% of the loan amount. The interest rate is negotiated between borrower and lender.

Eligibility Criteria: A rural area may include an area in any city or town that has a population of not more than 10,000 residents. Applicants must be unable to obtain sufficient credit elsewhere at reasonable rates to finance actual needs.

Funding: Loan authorization level for *direct* loans in FY2003: $779.1 million (includes emergency supplemental funding); FY2004: $1.032 billion; FY2005: $1.0 billion (est.). Loan subsidies for *direct* loans in FY2003: $88.3 million (includes emergency supplemental funding); FY2004: $34.4 million; FY2005: $90.0 million (est.). Loan authorization levels for *guaranteed* loans in FY2003: $3.6 million; FY2004: $75.0 million; FY2005: $75 million (est.).

Water and Waste Disposal Grants

Grants are made to public, quasi-public, and nonprofit associations as in the loan program. Grants are directed to projects serving the most financially needy communities. Grants are made to communities that have a median household income that falls below the higher of the poverty level or 100% of the state's non-metro household income. Grant amounts provide higher funding levels for projects in communities that have lower income levels but they may not exceed 75% of the eligible development costs of the project. In addition, between 1% and 3% of the grant funds appropriated each year for water and waste water is available for technical assistance and training to assist communities in identifying and evaluating alternative solutions to problems related to water and waste disposal, preparing applications, and improving operation and maintenance practices at existing facilities.

Statutory Authority: Section 306(a)(2) of the Consolidated Agriculture and Rural Development Act of 1972; 7 U.S.C. 1926.

Financing: Grants.

Eligibility Criteria: Grants are made only if needed to reduce user charges to a reasonable level. For a grant of up to 70% of eligible costs, service area median household income must be below the poverty level or below 80% of the State non-metropolitan median household income, whichever is higher.

Funding: FY2003: $622.4 million (includes emergency supplemental funding); FY2004: $544.0 million; FY2005: $346.0 million (est.).

Solid Waste Management Grants

Grants made to local and regional governments and to nonprofit organizations to provide technical assistance and training for the purposes of reducing or eliminating pollution of water resources and improving management of solid waste facilities.

> **Statutory Authority:** Section 310B(b) of the Consolidated Agriculture and Rural Development Act of 1972; 7 U.S.C. 1932(b).
> **Financing:** Grants.
> **Eligibility Criteria:** Assistance is available in rural areas and towns with a population of 10,000 or less.
> **Funding:** FY2003: $3.6 million; FY2004: $3.5 million; FY2005: $3.5 million (est.).

Emergency and Imminent Community Water Assistance Grants

The program assists rural communities that have had a significant decline in quantity or quality of drinking water. Grants can be made in rural areas and cities or towns with a population not in excess of 10,000 and a median household income not more than 100% of a State's non-metropolitan median household income. Grants may be made for 100% of project costs. The maximum grant is $500,000 when a significant decline in quantity or quality of water occurred within two years, or $75,000 to make emergency repairs and replacement of facilities on existing systems.

> **Statutory Authority:** Sections 306A and 306B of the Consolidated Agriculture and Rural Development Act of 1972; 7 U.S.C. 1926(a)(b).
> **Financing:** Grants.
> **Eligibility Criteria:** For declared emergencies and disasters and for communities facing actual or immanent drinking water shortages.
> **Funding:** The 2002 farm bill (P.L. 107-171) sets aside not less than 3% nor more than 5% of the total appropriated water and waste water funds for emergency community water assistance. Authorizes $35 million each year in additional funding for the program, FY2003-FY2007. For FY2003 $16.7 million (includes emergency supplemental funding); FY2004: $18.1 million; FY2005: $0 (est.).

Technical Assistance and Training (TAT) Grants

A percentage of the Water and Wastewater Grant Program is available each year to provide technical assistance for rural communities with a population of 10,000 or less. Grant funds may be used to assist communities and rural areas in identifying and evaluating solutions to water or wastewater problems, improving facility operation and maintenance activities, or preparing funding applications for water or wastewater treatment facility construction projects.

Statutory Authority: Section 306(a) of the Consolidated Agriculture and Rural Development Act of 1972; 7 U.S.C. 1989.
Financing: Grants.
Eligibility Criteria: Private, nonprofit organizations that have been granted tax-exempt status from the Internal Revenue Service may be eligible for grant funds provided they can demonstrate the ability, background, experience, legal authority, and actual capacity to provide technical assistance/training on a regional basis to small, rural communities.[18]
Funding: Formula funding based on the Water and Waste Water Grant appropriation for the current fiscal year.

Rural Water Circuit Rider Program

The program provides on-site technical assistance for the operation of rural water systems. Objective is to bring small public water systems into compliance with state and national environmental regulations. The program complements RUS loan supervision responsibilities. RUS contracts with the National Rural Water Association (NRWA) to provide this service in each state.

Statutory Authority: Section 306(a) of the Consolidated Agriculture and Rural Development Act of 1972; 7 U.S.C. 1989.
Financing: RUS has a management contract with National Rural Water Association which contracts with state water associations. State water associations operate the program.
Eligibility Criteria: Public water and waste water systems serving rural communities of 10,000 or less. Many states have further prioritized funding for very small communities.
Funding: Circuit rider staff positions are funded out of staffing authorizations for RUS.

USDA OFFICE OF COMMUNITY DEVELOPMENT

The Office of Community Development (OCD) is part of the USDA rural development mission area. OCD provides support for rural development activities through USDA Rural Development's field offices. The Office implements a range of special rural development initiatives, disseminates information about rural development strategies to rural development practitioners, and promotes communication and networking among rural development experts. OCD provides leadership and administrative oversight to two major programs: the Empowerment Zone/Enterprise Community Initiative and the Rural Economic Area Partnership Zones program.

Empowerment Zone/ Enterprise Community Initiative (EZ/EC)

The EZ/EC Program is a grant-making and tax-credit initiative whose objective is to revitalize low-income rural communities in a manner that attracts private sector investment. The purpose of the program is to demonstrate the value of innovative and strategic alliances between State, Federal, and local resources to improve the economic strength of rural communities. Through 3 rounds of competition, there are now 10 rural EZ areas and approximately 50 rural EC communities. The average poverty rate for designated EZ areas was approximately 35% in 2000 and the average unemployment rate approximately 14%.

Statutory Authority: Omnibus Budget Reconciliation Act of 1993, Title XIII, P.L.103-66; Taxpayer Relief Act of 1997, P.L.105-34; Agriculture, Rural Development, Food and Drug Administration, and Related Agencies Appropriations Act of 1999, P.L.105-277; 42 U.S.C. 11501, et seq.
Financing: Loans and grants.
Eligibility Criteria: A competitive program. A community must be a designated Empowerment Zone or Enterprise Community.
Funding: FY2003: $27.4 million; FY2004: $12.6 million; FY2005: $0(est). In addition to these funds, other USDA Rural Development program accounts are earmarked for EZ/EC communities. Round I Empowerment Zones/Enterprise Communities are funded over 10 years. Round II and III sites are funded predominantly through tax credits for employers within EZ/EC sites.

1. Round I EZ Sites (1994)
1. Kentucky Highlands
2. Mississippi Mid-Delta
3. Texas, Rio Grande

2. Round II EZ Sites- Authorized by Taxpayer Relief Act of 1997 (P.L.105-34)
1.Ogalala Sioux Reservation

2.Desert Communities, California
3. Southernmost, Illinois
4. Griggs-Steele, Southwest Georgia
5. Lewiston, Maine

3. Round III EZ Sites - Authorized by the Community Renewal Tax
Relief Act of 2000; Consolidated Appropriations Act of 2001
1. Aroostook County, Maine
2. Middle Rio Grande (FUTURO), Texas

Rural Economic Area Partnership Zones (REAP)

This is a pilot program for rural revitalization. The program assists rural
communities suffering from out-migration, economic crises, and geographic
isolation. Designated REAP Zones receive modest technical and financial
assistance from USDA as well as other federal agencies. REAP zones also
receive special consideration and preferences under regular Rural
Development loan and grant programs. Similar to the EZ/EC programs,
REAP zones engage in community-based, long-term planning and regularly
report on their progress using OCD's performance and benchmark reporting
system.

In 1995, two zones in North Dakota were initially designated to
participate in the REAP initiative. Subsequently, two areas in upstate New
York were added in 1999. In 2000, a rural area in Vermont was designated
as the fifth REAP Zone.

Statutory Authority: Presidential Memorandum dated August 5,
1993; variously dated Memoranda of Agreement; Agriculture, Rural
Development,
Food and Drug Administration, and Related Agencies Appropriations
Act of 2001 (P.L. 106-387).
Financing: Priority is given Zone applications submitted for funding
through the various programs administered by RUS, RHS, and RBS.
Eligibility Criteria: Designation by the Secretary as a REAP Zone.
Funding: FY2003: $10.2; FY2004: $10.6; FY2005: $0 (est.). (These
figures are approximate. Appropriators make earmarks for the REAP
program along with earmarks for the EZ/EC program). Earmarks to
other annual USDA appropriations also provide funding in addition to
the line item.

National Rural Development Partnership

The National Rural Development Partnership (NRDP) was authorized by the 2002 farm bill. The NRDP coordinates the efforts of public, private, and nonprofit groups interested in rural development issues. State Rural Development Councils, which exist in 36 states, are the major operative agents within the Partnership. The Partnership also includes the National Partnership Office which is housed in USDA and a National Rural Development Council. The latter consists of senior program managers from 40 federal agencies involved with rural development activities and national representatives of public interest and private sector organizations.

> **Statutory Authority:** Farm Security and Rural Investment Act of 2002 (Section 6201).
> **Financing:** State rural development offices provide matching funding to support partnership activities with State Rural Development Partnership Councils.
> **Eligibility Criteria:** State Rural Development Partnership Councils are composed of broadly representative pubic and private organizations.
> **Funding:** The 2002 farm bill (P.L. 107-171) authorized $10 million in each fiscal year FY2002-2007. No appropriations recommended/requested for FY2003-2005, although the Appropriators in FY2003-2004 encouraged the Secretary to support the NRDP through existing program funding.

REFERENCES

[1]   By virtue of its specific geographic targets, legislation authorizing the Appalachian Regional Commission, the Mississippi Delta Region, the Great Plains Region, and the Tennessee Valley Authority also has had a significant impact on rural development issues in these areas.

[2]   The Government Accountability Office identified 88 programs administered by 16 federal agencies that targeted rural development. See *Rural Development: Federal Programs that Focus on Rural American and its Economic Development*, GAO/RCED-89-56-BR, January 1989.

[3]   While the 1994 Act reorganized the administering agencies, the programs themselves predate the reorganization.

[4]   The Cooperative Marketing Act of 1926, the Agricultural Marketing Act of 1946, and the Agricultural Acts from 1931 to 1970 are also

significant for the role of agriculture within rural economies. While these statutes do not address rural development directly, they do provide marketing assistance for farmers and ranchers and thus, have contributed to rural welfare especially in those areas where agricultural production is also a significant economic focus.

[5]   See Section 301 of P.L. 87-128 as enacted on August 8, 1961, 75 Stat. 307.

[6]   USDA Rural Development (RUS, RBS, RHS) assumed administration of the former Farmers Home Administration's non-farm functions.

[7]   See *Housing the Poor: Federal Programs for Low-Income Families*, CRS Report RL30486, March, 2000.

[8]   National Rural Housing Coalition. *Recommendations to the Commission on Affordable and Healthy Facility Needs for Seniors in the 21st Century*, October 2001.

[9]   This goal, however, was not achieved until the early 1970s.

[10]   Modest housing is generally defined as housing costing less than the HUD Section 203(b) loan limits.

[11]   Unlike other RHS programs, the funding for Farm Labor Housing Program may be used in urban areas for nearby farm labor.

[12]   Other RBS-administered programs within the Rural Community Advancement Program are discussed in a later section.

[13]   FY2001 funds were provided in the *Agricultural Risk Protection Act of 2000* and the *Agriculture, Rural Development, Food and Drug Administration, and Related Agencies Appropriations Act, 2002 (P.L.106-387)*. Subsequent funding (FY2002-FY2007) is provided by the 2002 farm bill. In FY2004, appropriators blocked the mandatory funding and provided discretionary funds. For FY2005, the Administration has proposed cancelling the mandatory funds and providing discretionary funds.

[14]   Water and waste water programs are administered under the Rural Community Advancement Program and are discussed in the following section.

[15]   Includes loan authorization for guaranteed loans.

[16]   In FY2003, $29.8 million was transferred from the Rural Community Advancement Program account plus $5 million in unobligated funds. In FY2004, $27.8 was transferred from the Rural Community Advancement Program account.

[17]   For RBS loan performance data, see *Rural Development: Rural Business-Cooperative Service Business Loan Losses.* GAO/RCED, August, 1999.

[18] Since 1988, the Rural Community Assistance Program (RCAP), Inc.,
      in Leesburg, Virginia operates the Technitrain Program with grant
      funds under the TAT Grant Program. RCAP has operated the program
      since 1988. The program began with 180 communities and has
      expanded to around 500 communities in 47 States and Puerto Rico.

In: Rural Development ISBN 978-1-60021-161-4
Editors: T.Cowan, B.Foote, pp.45-139 © 2007 Nova Science Publishers, Inc.

Chapter 2

ECONOMIC DEVELOPMENT OPTIONS AND CONSTRAINTS IN REMOTE RURAL COUNTIES: A CASE STUDY OF THE GREAT PLAINS REGION[*]

Tadlock Cowan

SUMMARY

Although many rural areas fared relatively well over the past decade, there remain wide swathes of rural America that continue to decline. One of the more significant indicators of this selective decline is the population out-migration in remote rural areas of the Great Plains where agriculture and natural resource-based economies are predominant. Congress is concerned about theses areas and has proposed legislation to address the decline. Current conditions in much of the Great Plains suggest a continuing and deepening decline in the absence of new sources of competitive advantage. This is especially true for remote counties, which present distinct challenges for rural development policy in the 21st century. This report discusses socioeconomic characteristics and trends of 242 remote rural counties in seven states of the Great Plains region stretching from Texas to the Dakotas. Remote counties are defined here as those with populations

---

[*] Excerpted from CRS Report RL32372, dated April 29, 2004.

under six persons per square mile and on the extreme end of two widely used scales of rurality that categorize counties based on the extent to which they are influenced by urban areas or larger population centers. Appendices provide individual county level data on socioeconomic trends in population, education, employment, and income for the 242 remote counties.

Remote rural counties in the Great Plains experienced extensive population out-migration over the 1990s. With few employment alternatives in the private sector to replace the exodus of jobs from agriculture, mining, and timbering, remote counties are a particular concern to policymakers because the remaining population is disproportionately elderly, low-income, low-wage, and more dependent on agriculture and other natural resources than other rural areas. While the Great Plains area receives higher per capita federal funding than the country as a whole, most of the funds direct payments to individuals, e.g., Social Security, disability, farm subsidies rather than to capital-generating areas. This does not represent a difference from federal spending in non-metro areas generally, but in the Great Plains, programs that promote rural economic development may be even more important than in rural areas with more diversified economies, such as those within commuting distance to urban areas. The possibilities of regionally based solutions are discussed.

Most rural development researchers agree that the great diversity exhibited from one rural area to another makes crafting effective federal policy especially difficult. Contributing to this difficulty is the relative dearth of research that might help policymakers understand why some policies seem to work well in some rural areas and not so well in others. The United States Department of Agriculture classifications of rural areas into particular policy types and their dominant economic activity are two of the more widely cited efforts to impose some analytic order on the diversity of rural areas. Yet they still paint rural areas with a very broad brush. Understanding the particular characteristics and economic conditions of remote rural areas in the Great Plains may help legislators in making rural economic development policies to better deal with the circumstances of that region.

INTRODUCTION

Congressional interest in rural policy involves a wide range of issues, including agriculture, forestry, and mining production, community infrastructure, natural resource conservation and management, and socioeconomic development. Current challenges to and reform of existing federal rural policies are evolving in an environment of increasing concern about national competitiveness, new federal political strategies that devolve more power to state and local areas, deregulation of financial markets, budget constraints, and the increasing degree of separation between farm policies and rural economic development policies. Global socioeconomic changes are being felt especially in rural areas that have historically depended on natural resource based economies, including agriculture. A changing rural America is also producing pressures for different policies and raising new questions about the role Congress might play in shaping effective rural development policies for the future.

The Great Plains

Much of rural America lying outside urban commuting zones faces significant economic development challenges as the United States has increasingly become a largely urban/suburban and increasingly high-technology, bi-coastal economy.[1] Yet, the myriad problems facing rural America are often invisible to an urban and suburban world. Faced with weaknesses in the farm economy, persistent poverty, and the loss of manufacturing jobs to lower labor costs abroad, large expanses of rural America, especially those areas sparsely populated and remote from population centers, are falling farther behind their urban and suburban counterparts. This trend is not new nor are spatial inequalities a new phenomenon. Spatially unequal development characterizes virtually all countries in the developed world as well as the developing world. But these spatial inequalities have grown more pronounced in some U.S. regions over the past decade as the United States makes adjustments to the internationalization of markets and the division of labor. These patterns are visible throughout the United States. Nowhere is this perhaps more pronounced than in the Great Plains region, especially in that region's remote rural counties. (See definition and description of "remote rural areas" on page 5).

Remote rural areas of the Great Plains Region present distinctive spatial and socioeconomic dynamics that offer a stark example of the significant difficulties facing many other rural areas. Unlike many other rural areas, however, much of the Great Plains is undergoing significant population out-migration (see Figure 1). In this report, data on 242 remote rural counties in seven states of the Great Plains (Texas, Oklahoma, Nebraska, Kansas, South Dakota, North Dakota, and Montana) are examined. In Appendices C-I, individual remote county level data are provided on population change, household income, employment, and other socioeconomic variables.

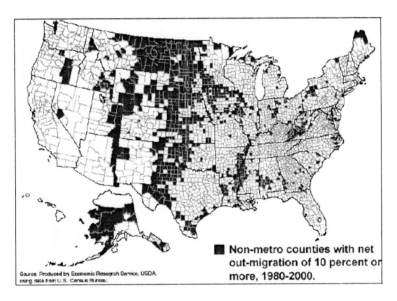

Figure 1. Demographic Decline in the Great Plains

The remote counties discussed here have experienced significant population loss, highlighting the fact the non-metro Great Plains counties have seen a relatively steady population decline. While the total population of these 242 counties is just under a million, representing a little over 12% of the non-metro population in the seven states, these counties might be regarded as an extreme case of more general phenomena accompanying widespread population decline in the region as a whole (see Table 1).

Table 1. Remote Great Plains County Population

State	State Population, 2000	State Non-Metro Population	Remote County Population	Percentage of Remote to State Non-Metro Population
Kansas	2.7 million	1.17 million	92,013	7.9%
Montana	902,195	692,486	275,393	39.8%
Nebraska	1.4 million	811,425	90,394	11.1%
North Dakota	642,200	347,724	131,877	37.9%
Oklahoma	3.4 million	1.35 million	29,965	2.2%
South Dakota	754,844	493,867	144,368	29.2%
Texas	20.8 million	3.16 million	209,699	6.6%
Total	30.5 million	8.0 million	973,709	12.2%

Source: Census 2000, Bureau of the Census, U.S. Department of Commerce.

As used here, the Great Plains region includes parts or all of Texas, Oklahoma, Nebraska, Kansas, North Dakota, South Dakota, and Montana stretching from central Texas to the Canadian border. Cycles of growth and decline have long characterized the region. In the late 1870s and early 1880s, an abnormal abundance of rain led many settlers to the region only to experience, a few years later, the blizzards of 1887 followed by a decade of withering drought. Periods of drought and depression lasted until the beginning of the 20th century, which ushered in a period of high agricultural commodity prices and good crop years that lasted through the first World War.[2] Following the Depression and World War II, another period of strong growth in the agricultural sector again made the Great Plains an economically competitive region. Since then, the steady decline in numbers of farms and the limited creation of non-farm jobs has left the region searching for new ways to rejuvenate local economies.

Over 60% of the counties in the Great Plains region had population declines from 1990-2000. In North Dakota, the state as a whole had a negative growth rate while the United States grew at an average of over 13% between 1990-2000. As younger persons migrate from many of these areas in the Great Plains, the elderly population increases proportionately, the tax base dwindles, public services decline, employers close shop, and small communities disappear. When Frederick Jackson Turner presented his landmark essay, *The Significance of the Frontier in American History*, to the American Historical Association at the Chicago World's Fair in 1893, an area of 6 or fewer persons was the defining criterion of frontier territory. Despite the large population growth of the U.S. during the 20th century, there are remote rural areas that have fewer persons living there today than lived there in 1890.[3]

These counties are also more dependent on farming than other non-metropolitan counties. While non-metro counties in general suffer higher rates of poverty than metro-counties, have lower wages than metro areas, low population densities, and/or less diversified economies, these 242 counties may fall into a distinct category that warrants special attention from policymakers. Although other states may have low-density rural areas and significant out-migration (e.g., Delta South and Central Appalachia), the remote rural areas of the Great Plains represent a distinct geographic region in the central part of the United States where farming is still important, out-migration is significant , employment opportunities are limited, environmental amenities are few, and the challenges of rural economic development particularly significant.

Rural Definitions

Rural areas, when compared to urban and suburban areas, are characterized by sparse populations, often great distances to population centers, and, accordingly, low scale efficiencies that make the provision of public and private services costly. Rural areas, according to the U.S. Census, comprise open country and settlements with fewer than 2,500 residents. The formal definition of rural is essentially a residual category: Rural areas consist of all territory outside of Census Bureau-defined *urbanized areas* and *urban clusters*. *Urbanized areas* have an urban nucleus of 50,000 or more people. They may or may not contain individual cities with 50,000 or more. In general, they must have a core with a population density of 1,000 persons per square mile and may contain adjoining territory with at least 500 persons per square mile. The same computerized procedures and population density criteria are used to identify *urban clusters* of at least 2,500 but less than 50,000 persons. This delineation of built-up territory and small towns and cities is new for the 2000 census.

Metro and non-metro areas are defined by the Office of Management and Budget. Metropolitan Statistical Areas and Micropolitan Statistical Areas are collectively referred to as Core Based Statistical Areas (CBSAs). Metro areas consist of (1) central counties with one or more urbanized areas and (2) outlying counties that are economically tied to the core counties as measured by worker commuting data. Outlying counties are included if 25% of workers living there commute to the core counties, or if 25% of the employment in the county consists of workers coming from the central counties. Non-metro counties are outside the boundaries of metro areas and are further subdivided into *micropolitan areas* centered on urban clusters of 10,000 or more residents, and all remaining "non-core" counties.[4]

Metropolitan and Micropolitan Statistical Areas do not equate to an urban-rural classification. All counties included in CBSAs, as well as "non-core"counties, contain both rural and urban territory and populations. Based on the most recent definitions above, there were 59.1 million *rural* residents of whom 49.2% lived in *non-metro counties* in 2000. There were 49.2 million non-metro county residents, 59% of whom lived in rural areas. Nationally, 17% of the population lived in non-metro counties and 21% lived in rural areas in 2000.[5] For programmatic as opposed to statistical analysis and demographic modeling purposes, however, "rural" most often refers to socioeconomic trends and conditions in non-metropolitan areas.[6] For example, statutory language in the 2002 farm bill (P.L.107-171, Sec. 6020) defines rural and rural area as any area other than an area with a city or town over 50,000 and the "urbanized area contiguous and adjacent to such a city or town." In this report, the terms rural, rural area, and non-metropolitan will be used interchangeably to refer to non-metropolitan areas unless otherwise specified to include the rural residents of metropolitan counties. Similarly, metropolitan and urban areas will be used interchangeably unless a specific reference is made to rural areas within metropolitan counties.[7]

Remote rural areas are defined in this report as (1) those with county population densities of 6 or fewer persons per square mile and (2) on the far end of a rural-urban continuum scale and a scale measuring the degree of urban influence on a rural area.[8] These remote counties are, arguably, even more vulnerable to the "tyranny of distance" when it comes to attracting residents and businesses that might provide the basis for creating new sources of economic growth and development. During the 1990s, some rural areas such as the Mountain West, while sparsely populated and with few large population centers, have seen significant population growth stemming from the presence of attractive environmental amenities. However, in the Great Plains region, containing a high proportion of farm-dependent counties, socioeconomic conditions have continued to decline.[9]

Background

An important issue for many rural areas is how to create new sources of rural competitive advantage beyond the traditional economies based on commodity agriculture, resource extraction, and peripheral manufacturing jobs. A recent survey indicates that, while state leaders regard rural economic development as vital to their respective states, actual legislative priorities have not placed rural development as a central issue of their states' legislative agendas. Approximately half the national sample of rural, suburban, and urban legislators reported that they personally dealt with rural issues. However, these legislators also noted that urban and suburban issues often took priority in the legislative agenda. They cited lack of opportunity for young people as the most important rural problem followed by decline of family farming. [10] Yet, when asked what legislative work occupied most of their agenda, 84% of the legislators reported that quality of education attracted the most legislative attention. Other areas cited were, the environment (70%), access to technology (69%), access to healthcare (64%) and access to transportation (59%). While some of these concerns are relevant to rural areas, economic development issues *per se* scored considerably lower on the legislative agenda: Only a third of the legislators cited lack of opportunity for young people as a key legislative concern.

The focus on rural oriented economic development policies has not been among the highest federal priorities, as measured by federal initiatives, since the 1960s and 1970s. Much national rural policy attempts either to reinvigorate traditional production spheres, such as agriculture, to build or improve physical infrastructure, and to create or preserve small businesses. Analysis by USDA's Economic Research Service (ERS)of data in the Consolidated Federal Funds Reports show that when compared to metropolitan areas, rural areas receive fewer federal funds per capita for funding that might be characterized as capital investment and more funds that are income support payments.[11] Although non-metro areas, in general, receive somewhat less funding per capita than metro areas, rural areas also often have even more limited access to important private investment resources because their remoteness and low population densities may increase project risks. Credit in rural areas, for example, can often be more expensive and offer fewer financial product options than those available in metropolitan areas. Rural communities also may have more difficulty in financing infrastructure projects and providing rental and middle income housing construction. Moreover, smaller rural communities often have limited taxing and repayment capacity. Large infrastructure projects, for example, may have the effect of raising taxes disproportionately for small rural communities, simply because there are fewer people over which costs can be spread.

Analysts have sometimes asked the question: "Why invest in rural America?"[12] America today is a suburban nation and becoming more so by the decade.[13] When the United States was younger, the rural sector was the "Frontier." In the early 20th century, it became the "Storehouse," the geography providing the raw commodities to support a growing urban industrial population.[14] In both periods, the rationale for investment and public support was clear. The importance of rural areas to the nation as a whole today appears to be more ambiguous.

In the 1960s and 1970s, the urban cores of many major U.S. cities, e.g., Detroit, Chicago, Cleveland, New York, Boston, Washington, D.C., were faced with the challenges of serious social and physical decline. Newspapers, news magazines, and television were awash in stories about urban decline, which generated a national debate about its causes and solutions. Over several years, Congress responded with a broad range of innovative polices aimed at reversing the deterioration and reinvigorating much of the country's older centers. The long-term decline of rural America, on the other hand, is happening relatively more quietly and often out of the public eye. Yet some would argue that rural challenges today are as great on a community level as were the challenges of cities 35 years ago. According to the General Accounting Office, the patchwork of programs that constitutes rural policy today is not the outcome of comprehensive and systematically crafted policy goals targeted to rural areas as much as it is extensions and modifications of programs designed for urban areas.[15] The agricultural and manufacturing sectors remain the primary foci in terms of amounts spent on rural areas. Some have questioned whether financial support to production agriculture necessarily translates into economically diverse and viable rural communities. Similarly, low-wage and low-skill manufacturing that often predominates in many rural areas may be unable to provide these areas with the capacity to rebuild local economies for the future, particularly with globalization and outsourcing of production.

Population Change in Non-Metro Areas During the 1990s

Approximately 49.2 million persons resided in non-metropolitan areas in 2003, 17.4% of the U.S. population.[16] After years of little or no growth in population, rural and small towns grew faster than suburban and urban areas in the 1970s. In the 1980s, however, this trend reversed with the 1981-1982 recession and the farm financial crisis, and a decline in number of retirees — a major source of rural population growth — moving to rural areas. A shift occurred again during the 1990s when most non-metro counties either increased their growth rates, shifted from a 1980s loss to a gain, or, continued a decline, although at a somewhat reduced rate. Population growth was highest in the Mountain West and lowest or non-existent in the Great Plains, Mississippi Delta, and Corn Belt. Non-metro counties adjoining metro areas accounted for almost two-thirds of all non-metro growth, increasing about 12% on average. Much of this growth stemmed from metro residents relocating to the adjoining non-metro areas and from other sources of immigration. Despite this net inflow of people from metro areas, the rate of net migration into rural areas, which had steadily increased during the early and mid-1990s, dropped to one-half of 1% during 1997-1999.[17] Because many low-growth farming areas, such as those in the Great Plains, lack the attraction of amenities such as those found in the Mountain West or Florida, it is hard to see how they will experience future population growth without new sources of employment.

During the 1990s, population remained stable or grew in those rural areas and small communities able to attract jobs in the service sector, the major source of employment growth in non-metro economies. Farm-dependent counties generally saw little or no growth or lost population in the 1990s. Foreign immigration was the major source of growth in the U.S. population, accounting for nearly 20% of the national non-metro growth in the1990s. While about 83% of all residents and nearly 90% of immigrants lived in urban areas in 2003, the immigration into rural and agricultural areas may be more socially significant than these broad data might suggest.

Immigration is important to farming, meat packing, and textiles; and immigrant professionals, e.g., physicians, also play an increasingly important role in many rural areas. Much of labor-intensive agriculture is located in the South and in geographically large western counties classified by the census as metropolitan areas. Crop production, fruit and vegetable farming, and meat packing industries are reliant on hired farm workers. Hispanics comprised 42% of hired farm workers in 2002.[18] Some are new immigrants from central Mexico and non-Spanish speaking Indians of southern Mexico and Guatemala. In the Upper Midwest, Mexicans and Mexican-Americans from the Rio Grande Valley along with a few middle-class Cubans and Puerto Ricans and other Latin Americans also reside. The majority of Hispanic immigrants in the Upper Midwest arrived to work in the region's new and expanding swine and turkey processing plants. In the Lower Midwest, many immigrants took jobs in the meat packing plants.[19]

THE DECLINING OPPORTUNITY STRUCTURE OF REMOTE RURAL AREAS OF THE GREAT PLAINS

Population loss throughout much of the rural and farming dependent areas of the Great Plains region has been persistent and continual for over 50 years. Out-migration of young residents and lower fertility rates of those who remain have led not only to population loss, but also to the increased proportion of the aging in the population remaining. When low population densities are added to this demographic mix, a picture of a slowly declining region emerges (see Table 2). The average population in the remote counties in all of the states but Montana had negative growth rates between 1990 and 2000 (Table 2). All the states but Montana had growth rates below the national average of approximately 13%.[20] Not only did North Dakota's remote counties have the lowest growth rate among the 7 states, the state average was negative as well. Population densities in the region, as measured by population per square mile, average less than a tenth of the average non-metro county average of slightly over 36 persons per square mile.

Table 2. Great Plains Population

	Average Remote County Population, 2000 (1)	Average Remote County Population Change, 1990-2000 (%)	Average State Population Change, 1990-2000 (%)(2)	Average Remote County Population Density (population per sq.mi)(3)	Average State Population Density (population per sq.mi) (4)
Kansas	3,173	-5.10	8.5	4.0	32.9
Montana	6,120	2.6	12.9	2.3	6.2
Nebraska	2,825	-6.1	8.4	2.7	22.3
North Dakota	3,768	-13.0	-1.2	3.5	9.3
Oklahoma	4,281	-10.0	9.7	4.0	50.3
South Dakota	4,125	-0.4	8.5	3.2	9.9
Texas	3,554	-1.0	22.8	2.8	79.6

Sources: Census 2000, Bureau of the Census; USDA-Economic Research Service; Bureau of Economic Analysis. (1)Remote counties are defined as those with county population densities of 6 or fewer persons per square mile and on the far end of a rural-urban continuum scale and a scale measuring the degree of urban influence on a rural area. (See Appendix A). (2)Average U.S. Population Change, 1990-2000 is 13.1%; (3)Average U.S. non-metro-county population density (2000) is 36.3 persons per square mile; (4) Includes a state's metropolitan areas.

Persons aged 65 and over comprise about 12% of the total U.S. population. For the remote counties of the Great Plains region, this age group makes up 16-21% of the counties' population (see Table 3). A proportionately higher elderly population produces significant challenges for rural areas, perhaps most important is providing health care services. The migration from rural areas also displays distinctive patterns. The number of non-metro counties with decreasing population rose from 600 from 1990-1995 to 855 in 1999 suggesting that there may be growing momentum for population loss.[21] Much of this more recent increase in rural out-migration (1997-1999) occurred among college graduates, with those moving out in numbers nearly equal to those moving in for the first time since the early 1990s.[22] Whether this pattern also characterized the remote counties is not clear. Average state high school graduation rates in the Great Plains states, with the exception of Texas, exceed the national average. For remote rural counties, the percentage of high school graduates is somewhat lower in North Dakota, South Dakota, and Texas than either their state or national averages. For those with bachelors degrees or higher, the Great Plains states are slightly below national averages while their remote counties are substantially below both averages.

Table 3. Great Plains Age and Education Structure, 2000

	Average Remote County Population 65 and older (%)	Average State Population 65 and older (%)	Average Remote County High-School graduates, 25 and older (%)	Average State High-School graduates, 25 and older (%)	Average Remote County Bachelors degree or higher (%)	Average State Bachelors degree or higher (%)
Kansas	21.2	13.3	84.1	86.0	17.0	25.8
Montana	16.4	13.4	83.1	87.2	17.9	24.4
Nebraska	20.1	13.6	86.7	86.6	16.0	23.7
North Dakota	21.3	14.7	77.3	83.9	14.5	22.0
Oklahoma	20.0	13.2	80.8	80.6	17.5	20.3
South Dakota	17.6	14.3	78.2	84.6	14.4	21.5
Texas	16.9	9.9	69.6	75.7	15.5	23.2
United States		12.4		80.4		24.4

Sources: Census 2000, Bureau of the Census, U.S. Department of Commerce.

Based on per capita income levels, many of the poorest counties in the United States are in very rural, farming-dependent counties.[23] Only one county among the poorest 50 counties is a metropolitan county. Eleven of the 20 poorest counties in the United States are located in remote counties in Nebraska, and North and South Dakota (see Table 4). Other high-poverty counties are located in the South and Appalachia and in areas where there is a high proportion of racial minorities.[24]

Table 4. Poor Great Plains County Rankings (1999)

County/State	Rank (1)	Rural-Urban Continuum Code (2)	Urban Influence Code (3)	Per Capita Income (4)(5)	
Loup, Nebraska	1	9	9	$	4,896
McPherson, Nebraska	2	9	9	$	6,940
Keya Paha, Nebraska	5	9	9	$	9,993
Ziebach, South Dakota	6	9	9	$	10,390
Arthur, Nebraska	7	9	9	$	10,655
Todd, South Dakota	10	9	9	$	10,920
Sioux, North Dakota	11	9	9	$	11,023
Sioux, Nebraska	12	9	9	$	11,147
Shannon, South Dakota	13	7	8	$	11,351
Blaine, Nebraska	16	9	9	$	11,576
Slope, North Dakota	19	9	9	$	12,097

Source: Bureau of Economic Analysis; USDA Economic Research Service
(1) Rank is among the 3,141 counties in the Nation, with 1 being the county with the lowest per capita income.
(2) (3) See Appendix A for a discussion of these ERS scales
(4) U.S. per capita income, 1999=$28,543
(5) Non-metro per capita income, 2000=$19,850

Average poverty and unemployment rates are higher in rural areas than in urban areas. The non-metro poverty rate declined from a high of 17.1 in 1993 to a record low of 13.4 in 2000. By 2001, the non-metro poverty rate had increased to14.2% while for metro areas the rate was 11.1%.[25] The remote rural counties of the Great Plains often had higher rates of poverty than non-metro areas as a whole and substantially lower median household incomes (see Table 5). It should be noted, however, that North Dakota, South Dakota, Oklahoma, and Montana are also home to significant Native American populations, who rank among the poorest in the nation, with unemployment rates often exceeding 50% on some reservations.

Table 5. Remote County Household Income, Poverty, and Unemployment Rates, 2000-2001

	Median Remote County Household Income	Median State Household Income	Average Remote County Poverty Rate(%) (1)	Average State Poverty Rate (%)	Average Remote County Unemployment Rate (%) (2)	Average State Unemployment Rate (%) (2)
Kansas	$ 32,856	$ 40,624	11.3	9.9	2.6	4.3
Montana	$ 29,426	$ 33,024	17.4	14.6	4.8	4.6
Nebraska	$ 29,241	$ 39,250	13.9	9.7	2.5	3.1
North Dakota	$ 29,169	$ 34,604	15.0	11.9	3.4	2.8
Oklahoma	$ 30,889	$ 33,400	13.7	14.7	2.6	3.8
South Dakota	$ 28,010	$ 35,282	22.3	13.2	5.1	3.3
Texas	$ 29,569	$ 39,927	18.4	15.4	3.6	4.9
United States	$ 41,944		13.4		4.8%	

Sources: U.S. Department of Commerce, Bureau of the Census; U.S. Department of Labor, Bureau of Labor Statistics; USDA, Economic Research Service; U.S. Department of Commerce, Bureau of Economic Analysis.
(1) U.S. average, 12.4%
(2) These data are for 2001

HUMAN CAPITAL ISSUES IN REMOTE RURAL AREAS

Human capital refers generally to the level of education and training of a defined group (e.g., population or labor force) and is important because of the direct relationship between educational attainment and earnings.[26] The demand for workers with at least some postsecondary education has been increasing in recent decades and is projected to rise at an above average rate in coming years.[27] Compared to metro areas, rural areas are chronically short of human capital.[28] As Table 3 shows, remote counties in the Great Plains have many fewer residents with a bachelors degree than the nation as a whole. While the national average for a bachelors degree or higher is

24.4%, the metropolitan rate is higher still at 29.1%. For remote rural counties in the Great Plains, the average is about 16%, about the same as the U.S. average for all non-metro counties in 2000. High-school graduation rates in non-metro areas have improved over the decade. Data from the Census of Population, calculated by USDA's Economic Research Service, showed that in 2000, only 23.2% of persons 25 and over had less than a high school education, down from 31.2% in 1990.

It would be misleading to attribute the economic problems of remote rural economies to a comparatively low-skilled population alone. As Table 5 shows, the unemployment rates in remote counties, with the exception of South Dakota, are actually lower than the national average. These relatively low unemployment rates suggest that rural workers may suffer more from low-wage employment and underemployment than they do from unemployment. This in part, reflects the types of industries that dominate rural areas: peripheral manufacturing, extractive industries, and low-wage service sector jobs.[29] Even highly skilled rural workers however, earn lower wages than their urban counterparts.[30] In 2000, the percentage of non-metro adults 25 and older with a high school diploma was higher in non-metro areas than in metro areas (35.5% vs. 26.9%), although only 15.5 percent of non-metro adults 25 and older held bachelors degrees compared to 26.6 of metro residents 25 and older.[31] According to data from the Rural Sociological Society Task Force on Rural Poverty, at every level of education, average earnings and income are lower in non-metro than in metro areas.[32]

The low reported unemployment rates could also suggest that, due to limited opportunities, rural workers have dropped out or never entered the workforce and are, accordingly, not officially counted as unemployed. This is undoubtedly true, but such bias in measuring unemployment is likely equally true for metropolitan areas as well, even though the composition of available employment differs. The non-farm employment change in remote counties shown in Table 6 gives a picture of a slow growth area relative to the state as a whole. This could be discouraging to would-be workers choosing areas to which they might migrate. There is also evidence to suggest that some rural labor market groups, such as underemployed workers and discouraged workers, respond less to business cycle movements. Therefore, an expansion may be less likely to benefit these individuals in rural areas than in urban areas.[33] Evidence, however, is lacking that unemployment counts in rural areas are any less or any more accurate than those for metro areas.

One substantive implication seems clear: rural people may suffer less from unemployment than from myriad forms of underemployment, e.g., working less than full time.[34] While average rates of high school graduation increased in rural areas over the 1990s, earnings per job did not. The inflation adjusted rural-urban earnings gap (as opposed to total income) was over 30% greater in 1995 than it was in 1977.[35] There are also other possible reasons for this gap including the lower likelihood of non-metro workers moving out of low wage jobs than central city residents, greater involuntary part-time work among non-metro workers, higher proportion of non-metro workers in minimum wage jobs (12% vs. 7%), and higher rates of underemployment and unemployment among women compared to metro areas.[36] Some recent research also suggests that an increased demand for unskilled, largely Hispanic labor may have contributed to lower wages for skilled workers (largely men with high school education) in some rural areas. Results from this research indicated that increased labor demand favored skilled and professional workers overall but favored unskilled workers in some rural industries, e.g., meatpacking.[37]

Real non-metro per capita income (in 1996 dollars) — as opposed to earnings alone — increased 2.4% between 1995-96 compared to 2.1% in metro areas. The ratio of non-metro to metro income improved from 71.2% in 1995 to 71.4% in 1996.[38] Table 6 shows that the average wage per non-farm job in remote counties is substantially lower than the average for their respective state's as a whole and that remote county per capita income change was substantially lower than for their respective states with the exception of North Dakota. Moreover, while per capita income grew by over 21% from 1990-2000 in the United States as a whole, per capita income grew in Great Plains remote counties on average by only about 5%.

Although low-wage employment is not unique to rural areas, it does make up a significant portion of all rural jobs. In a detailed examination of low-wage rural employment, USDA's Economic Research Service identified 465 counties they defined as low-wage counties.[39] A county was defined as low-wage if it fell into the top quintile of rural counties ranked by the share of wage and salary workers in low-wage industries. While federally-defined poverty, unemployment, and population growth rates in low-wage counties did not differ significantly from other rural counties, low-wage counties were characterized by a different mix of jobs. Industries that tend to pay well on average are less likely to be located in low-wage counties and jobs pay less on average than similar jobs elsewhere. With less diverse economies to begin with, employers in low-wage counties also have little competition in setting prevailing wage rates. Unsurprisingly, low-wage counties have relatively small numbers of workers and a larger proportion of older, less educated workers. These factors, coupled with out-migration of younger, higher skilled workers, make it difficult to attract the more technologically advanced production sectors that might improve both the wage structure and the level of work skills.

Table 6. Remote County Employment Structure

	Remote County Average Wage per non-Farm Job, 2000	State Average Wage per non-Farm Job, 2000	Remote County Private Non-Farm Employment Change, 1990-1999 (%)	Average State Private Non-Farm Employment Change, 1990-1999 (%)	Average Remote County Per Capita Income Change, 1990-2000 (%)	Average State Per Capita Income Change, 1990-2000 (%)
Montana	$ 20,111	$ 24,274	19.1	30.0	4.6	10.2
Nebraska	$ 17,842	$ 27,692	17.5	25.0	-11.1	16.0
North Dakota	$ 20,777	$ 24,683	22.8	27.3	22.7	18.2
Oklahoma	$ 20,928	$ 26,988	12.7	24.5	0.7	10.8
South Dakota	$ 19,194	$ 24,802	32.0	37.2	17.1	21.4
Texas	$ 22,540	$ 34,941	26.2	32.4	6.0	20.7
United States		$ 35,323		18.4		21.3

Sources: U.S. Department of Commerce, Bureau of the Census; U.S. Department of Labor, Bureau of Labor Statistics; USDA, Economic Research Service; U.S. Department of Commerce, Bureau of Economic Analysis.

The northern Great Plains region has the largest cluster of low-wage counties. Nearly half are located in North and South Dakota and Nebraska. Low-wages and small per capita income growth characterize both low-wage counties and remote counties as defined here. Counties remote from metro centers and with small pools of skilled workers are not positioned to attract employers who need access to suppliers and customers. The absence of skilled workers is also reflected in the lack of economic diversity in low-wage counties. Nearly half of the 465 low-wage counties analyzed by ERS are also classified in the county typology in Appendix A, Table 7 as "farming-dependent." Most of these are also located in the northern Great Plains region. This is not to imply that farm-employment *per se* is the source of the low-wages. Rather, farm-dependent counties may be low-wage because they are remote, have low population densities, and/or have been unable to diversify their economies outside the traditional agriculture economy. Few low-wage counties are dependent on manufacturing which generally pays higher wages in rural counties compared to other rural employment options.[40] Residents of remote counties without diverse economies simply have very limited opportunities to improve education and skill levels beyond that required for rudimentary, entry level jobs. The primary economic base of remote rural areas — farming/ranching, mining, forestry, and oil and gas extraction — is also prone to boom-bust cycles that not only make earning a living difficult, but may also help explain the frequent out-migration.

Six of the 10 industries with the largest share of employment in low-wage counties were classified as low-wage industries. The 10 largest low-wage industries all have greater shares of employment in low-wage counties than in other non-metro counties. Lower wages also exist within each industry so that the same job pays less in a low-wage county than in other non-metro counties. For example, medical doctors and health care personnel in low-wage counties earn on average 28% less than comparable workers in rural medical clinics elsewhere. Appendix B presents data on the top 25 industries in rural counties and compares low-wage counties with other rural counties.[41]

While many remote counties are poor and low-wage, the dynamics that drive these two processes are not necessarily the same. Of the 465 counties that ERS identified as low-wage, only about one-third were persistently poor and only about one-third of the persistently poor counties were low-wage.[42] This relation suggests that the underlying economic and social conditions associated with significant poverty and low-wages may differ. If low-wage earnings employment were the sole source of poverty, one would expect low-wage counties to have higher poverty rates, on average, than non low-wage counties. Conversely, one might expect persistently poor counties to be mostly low-wage counties. While it is substantially true that the economies of rural America were historically grounded in a manufacturing and agricultural base that produces large numbers of low-wage jobs, changes over the last 50 years have resulted in fewer agricultural jobs and more in services. Still, these jobs pay lower wages on average than similar sectoral employment in urban areas.

In the Great Plains region, remote, low-density counties are low-wage counties. The Great Plains region and, to some extent, the greater Midwestern region, also depends heavily on large-scale, capital-intensive agricultural production. Thirty of the 242 remote rural counties are in the leading 100 U.S. counties in total acreage in cropland.[43] Policies that have largely targeted farm household income have not produced an economic reversal in this region. *The evidence of demographic and socioeconomic trends in the Great Plains suggests to many observers that a continuing reliance on commodity agriculture to the exclusion of other, better paying employment, may be a formula for continuing population out-migration, fewer service and retail centers, and declining living standards for many rural households in the non-farming sector.* With significant changes occurring as well in the structure of agriculture leading to further concentration in production, non-farm employment, and closer ties between population centers and rural areas, more attention to regional solutions may hold greater promise for the Great Plains in the intermediate term than the traditional state or county-based solutions alone.

FEDERAL FUNDING IN THE GREAT PLAINS

This section relies on 1995 Bureau of the Census data generated by USDA's Economic Research Service.[44] The data focused on funding for 750 federal programs that were traceable to the county level. These programs accounted for 88% of all federal funds including funding to individuals, to businesses, and to public entities. Based on an examination of all federal funds received in FY1995, the Great Plains received more federal funds, per capita, than the country as a whole. (The Great Plains region as defined in the ERS report, in addition to the 7 states discussed in this report, also includes parts of eastern Wyoming, Colorado, New Mexico and western Minnesota). Per capita funds were 10% higher in the region ($5,447) than in the Nation as a whole ($4,973). Most of these funds were direct payments to individuals, e.g., Social Security and disability, farm subsidies, salaries, wages, and procurement contracts. Compared to the Nation as a whole, the region gets relatively more funding from such programs as agriculture and natural resource payments, defense and space, and community resource programs. While retirement and disability payments in the Great Plains account for slightly less than the Nation as a whole (32% vs. 34%), these payments are significant to local economies because of the relatively high percentages of elderly and disabled in the non-metro population (See Table 4 above and Appendices C-I)).

Non-metro counties rather than metro counties accounted for the greater levels of federal funding for the Great Plains as compared to the national average. Federal funding to non-metro counties in the Great Plains was 19% more per capita than for non-metro counties nationally and was 8% more per capita for Great Plains' metro counties compared to all metro counties. This difference in non-metro funding is explained by the relatively high level of payments to individuals in farm-dependent counties. Over half (277) of the 477 Great Plains counties were farm-dependent. The per capita annual government payments to these farm-dependent counties was $6,196. The 26 ERS-defined government-dependent counties and the 62 persistent poverty counties received $6,462 and $5,886 per capita, respectively.[45] The relatively few non-metro counties receiving low federal payments per capita tended to be (1) near or adjacent to metro counties, (2) specialize in mining, and (3) have little farming or were involved mostly in ranching operations.

Aside from retirement, disability, wages, salaries, and contracts, non-metro areas of the Great Plains are distinguished in their receipt of "other" direct payments, which include farm payments. Nationally, "other" direct payments to non-metro counties account for only 2% of federal funds and direct loans only about 4% of federal funds. For Great Plains non-metro counties, "other" direct payments account for 10% of funds and direct loans account for 7% of federal receipts. Farm-dependent counties in the Great Plains receive 17% of their total federal funds from non-farm "other" direct payments, and 12% from direct loans (farm and non-farm).

Federal funding in the Great Plains region may raise questions about the effectiveness of certain rural development strategies or human capital improvements in the region. The region receives higher per capita funding than the nation as a whole for elementary and secondary education, for higher education, and for agricultural and natural resource programs. Much of this latter funding goes to farm-dependent counties which are also disproportionately remote counties. Yet, socioeconomic data indicates that, despite these programs, there has not been a strong positive effect in improving the social welfare for most of the residents of these counties (See Appendices C-I). There are a number of possible explanations. In other rural economies outside the Great Plains, the agricultural sector may be important, but it is situated in an overall economy that is more diverse, thus the agricultural income and employment multiplier effects tend to be diluted in the local economy. In the Great Plains region, direct federal payments for agriculture and community resources are significant within the local economy, even more so in remote counties.[46] Yet, this funding, as an income transfer, appears to have a generally weak effect in building local economic development capacity. Given that farm payments in the late 1990s provided as much as 60% of farm household incomes in some areas of the United States, one can clearly understand their importance to certain families. Because the populations are so small in remote Great Plains counties, however, a few farm households receiving disproportionately higher direct farm payments may give a very misleading impression about per capita income and earnings for the county as a whole. The fact that farming-dependency, remoteness, and poverty are intertwined within a particular county may suggest a distinctive confluence of socioeconomic forces that limit the development potential of these areas.

Federal payments make up a relatively significant share of personal income in the Great Plains. There are also few employment alternatives in the private sector to replace the exodus of jobs from agriculture and mining. Non-metro counties in general and remote counties of the Great Plains in particular have relatively high proportions of elderly and disabled residents, making the federal funds they receive significantly more important to rural residents and communities. Changes in Medicare, federal transportation policies, or agricultural/natural resource programs may, in the absence of employment alternatives, may have a significantly greater effect in the Great Plains than in other regions.

Nationally, the counties with the highest job growth in the 1990s were service-based and government based counties. From 1995-1998 these counties grew at a rate of approximately 1.2%. Mining-dependent counties grew at about 0.7% and manufacturing-dependent counties grew at approximately 0.5% during that period. Job growth was about 0.25% in farm-dependent counties. While the number of farm-dependent counties has decreased nationally from over 60% of non-metro counties in 1950 to about 15% in 2000, most of the counties that remain dependent on agriculture are in the Great Plains region, along with Minnesota and Iowa.

POLICY OPTIONS FOR REMOTE RURAL AREAS OF THE GREAT PLAINS

Current strategies for rural economic development in the Great Plains are not substantially different from the strategies used in other rural regions. Given the distinctiveness of the problems facing remote rural areas in the region, the effectiveness of current government policies is an important question. It might be impractical to suggest that the tremendous diversity characterizing rural America also implies that separate federal policies should be created for each distinctive rural area. The range of existing federal loans and grants designed to create or support small businesses, improve rural infrastructure, and address the most pressing needs of low-income populations in housing, sewerage, and water have made important contributions to rural residents. One issue that Congress may ultimately face is whether such programs will provide needed economic stimulus in an internationalized economy where U.S. rural areas not only compete with each other, but increasingly with foreign countries, whose labor costs, land, and various regulatory structures may give them advantages.

Virtually any state can point to numerous small-scale, public and private sector rural economic development initiatives achieving notable successes within their borders. New jobs have been created, existing jobs retained, worker skills upgraded, new infrastructure built, and small rural communities revitalized based on a mix of agriculture, small-businesses, public service employment, and entrepreneurial activity. A larger number of remote rural communities, however, either are only holding their own or losing ground in terms of quality of life that the area's existing economic structure can provide. While their socioeconomic characteristics and histories are quite different, they appear to pose some seemingly intractable development problems — intractable in the sense that the current set of federal rural policies do not seem to create the necessary local capacities to effect a significant change in social well-being. The remote rural areas of the Great Plains reveal these challenging development problems, perhaps to a greater extent than any other region of the United States. Manufacturers find remoteness a significant barrier to relocating facilities; the growth and demand for business and professional services is greatest in urban areas; climate and landscape in the Great Plains offer little to encourage growth of tourism-related development. The result is very few well-paid jobs to replace lost employment in traditional sectors.

One overarching strategy that seems to be emerging is to consider rural economic development in regional terms. New regional development alliances are appearing throughout the United States (discussed below). One reason they may be doing so now is because the long-standing patterns of poverty and economic distress that characterize the Northern Great Plains, as well as other relatively impoverished and socially isolated areas, have not responded as successfully to the existing range of economic development programs as have other rural areas. Second, agricultural production, perhaps more so than in other regions, is central to the economies of remote Great Plains counties. But the summary of research presented here suggests that unless new initiatives in integrating agriculture and rural development strategies are successful, even the long-standing importance of that sector may not reverse the trends now shaping the Great Plains region. Finally, the remoteness of so much of the Great Plains is a significant factor in frustrating even the most optimistic development strategies.

A Continuing Role for Agriculture?

It appears that the agriculture-dependent counties of the Great Plains region generally and remote counties in particular may have stark choices before them. These areas may remain in agriculture because non-agricultural development strategies have not been as successful in the Great Plains region as they have been in other parts of the United States. This is so even though, on a per capita basis, the counties of the Great Plains receive a relatively high level of federal funds. Population in this area is declining because modern agriculture does not provide high-wage jobs and there are few choices for non-farm work. What non-farm work is available is generally low-skilled and/or pays less than comparable work in urban areas.

Single-sector dominated economies are highly vulnerable to external shocks, e.g., global price declines for raw agricultural commodities, cheaper sourcing sites for timber and minerals. Even in local economies where tourism is important, shifts in vacation destinations can damage businesses and related tax revenues. More economically diverse areas weather macro-economic shocks better. With most U.S. farm households heavily dependent on off-farm income, those in rural areas without diversified economies are at an increasing disadvantage.[47] This disadvantage is especially severe for farm-dependent counties. If one assumes that agriculture will remain a significant economic sector in the Great Plains for the foreseeable future, successful rural development strategies may need to consider the extent to which agriculture can impede or promote more diverse rural economies. Rather than focusing largely on policies that aim at bulk production of agricultural commodities, policymakers may begin to evaluate non-traditional ways in which agriculture might contribute to healthy rural economies. In many areas of the country, it may be the case that a healthy non-farm rural economy will become the most effective means of maintaining communities and the future sustainability of the farm population. Rural development researchers and others observe that because less than 2% of rural residents identify farming as their primary occupation, efforts to stimulate economic development through agriculture may not directly address the large majority of the population who have few if any substantial ties to agriculture. The Great Plains might arguably be one area of the United States where a greater emphasis on non-farm policies might have the effect of integrating agriculture in ways that enhance the overall regional economy.[48]

As discussed above, farming-dependent counties are disproportionately represented among remote and low-wage/income counties. Few development strategies that focus on the non-farm sector have had pronounced positive effects in the Great Plains. Other variables limit the economic development opportunities of the region. First, the remoteness of the region makes it unlikely that advanced manufacturing facilities will locate there. Many high-technology manufacturing enterprises increasingly choose to locate near suppliers or their customer base. They also rely on business and professional services that are almost non-existent in remote rural areas. Second, there are fewer natural environmental amenities such as are found in the Mountain West or in many retirement destination areas. The Plains may hold their own beauty to many, but the climate may not be conducive to strategies that rely on attracting and retaining high-paying manufacturing firms. With estimates as high as 300,000 U.S. communities vying for 15,000 firms reportedly seeking to relocate, remote areas of the Great Plains face a serious challenge.

Structural Changes in Agriculture

Changes in agriculture have led some analysts to suggest new policy considerations for the Great Plains.[49] Long-standing trends toward fewer, larger, and more specialized commercial farms and ranches in the United States (horizontal integration) are well documented. Not only have these trends been observed for many years, recent data suggest they may be accelerating as pressures increase from global competitors and as new agricultural technologies continue to reinforce the substitution of capital for labor. Some researchers have argued that current trends are leading to a farm structure where 10,000 acre corn farms may soon become the economically efficient size unit for that commodity.[50] Rapid and increasing consolidation and coordination and deepening vertical integration in agriculture are indicators of a more fundamental restructuring occurring in the global food and fiber system today. A growing share of commodity producers, mostly within animal production currently, are joining supply chains.[51] A supply chain is a tightly organized production system formed by agribusiness firms that, in its most coordinated form, could potentially link each step of food production from proprietary genetic material to the grocery shelf. Broiler production is the exemplar of this trend. Approximately 40 firms now contract to produce 97% of all broilers. These trends are appearing increasingly in pork production and are beginning in cash grains.

A distinguishing characteristic of supply chains is their reliance on contractual agreements, licenses, joint ventures, integrated ownership, and other business arrangements with different segments of the agro-food system. These alliances with producers may permit contracting firms to by-pass more traditional commodity markets. To better insulate themselves from price volatility and dwindling markets, many commodity producers are abandoning their independent operations and adopting contract commodity production and marketing arrangements with agribusiness firms. According to the USDA's Economic Research Service, about 35% of the total value of U.S. agricultural production in 1998 was produced under some form of contractual arrangement.[52] Over half of large family farms are involved in some form of contracting and these farms accounted for over 66% of the total value of commodities under contract.[53] Over 90% of the total value of contract production was in 10 commodity groups: soybeans, corn, fruit, vegetable, nursery, cotton, cattle, hogs, poultry, and dairy.

The growth of supply chains has implications for remote Great Plains counties because of their potential for creating geographically specific production sectors in agriculture that some observers have characterized as a hub, spoke, and wedge cluster.[54] For example, a livestock-processing plant located at a hub is built near livestock-feeding operations. These feeding operations are supplied by mills drawing their grain and oilseed through transportation and communication spokes connecting crop production "wedges" in the periphery. Few clusters may be needed to supply the demand. Many farming areas that might wish to become a "hub" may not be able to assemble the necessary capital and managerial services to do so. The characteristics of remote rural counties of the Great Plains might make the region compatible with large-scale animal operations. On the other hand, it is possible that only a relatively few hubs will be economically feasible under supply chain arrangements. Other countries, e.g., Canada, may also become increasingly competitive as supply hubs. Some industry observers believe that under a supply chain arrangement, for example, 50 or fewer pork producers and 12 state-of-the-art packing plants could, in the near future, supply the entire U.S. pork market.[55] Integrated ownership of a supply hub could also displace resources from traditional farms and rural areas.[56]

The trends toward supply chains and integrated agro-food chains may pose problems for remote, farm-dependent areas in the Great Plains. A different kind of agriculture, however, one that is not oriented exclusively to the production of bulk commodities, may have some potential in revitalizing the Great Plains. A recent workshop on integrating agriculture into rural development strategies pointed to many new agricultural ventures that have been successful.[57] They tend to be based on small-scale entrepreneurship, new marketing strategies, and the needs of rural people and consumers. New opportunities in value-added production may also offer remote counties in the Great Plains a way to build production agriculture into new economic development strategies.[58] Given the role that the land-grant system plays in the "treadmill of production," Congress may also consider ways of making publicly funded agricultural research more responsive to the needs of new agricultural enterprises, e.g., non-traditional crops, alternative production systems, marketing strategies for value-added agricultural development. With the aging of existing farm owner/operators, new opportunities for beginning farmers may offer other ways to revitalize the relation between agriculture and rural economic development.[59] This is not to suggest that large-scale agriculture will cease to have a significant role in the Great Plains. The Great Plains may actually offer new competitive advantages for this sector through innovations in environmental control and management technologies directed toward the agricultural sector.

It has long been a central statement of hope and optimism that support for agriculture would translate into strong, sustainable rural communities. When agriculture dominated the rural economy in the early 20th century, this was, in large part, true. But, with the exception of some areas of the United States, agriculture plays a relatively small role in most rural economies now. Modernizing agriculture has traditionally meant improving production; and improving production has been defined almost exclusively as increasing output per unit. Supported by the land-grant university system, research into ever-increasing production efficiency has also been associated with ever increasing scales of production. Larger and larger farms and ranches capable of taking advantage of scale efficiencies were often seen as a necessary correlate to technologically driven agriculture. That model has been captured most succinctly in Willard Cochrane's analogy of the "treadmill of production."[60] Output-enhancing research benefits consumers in lowering the price of food, but it can be argued it does so at the expense of the producer who must adopt the newest output-enhancing research on ever-shrinking profit margins.

Overcoming Remoteness: An Interstate Skyway System

While other rural areas in the United States may be at some distance from urban areas or even sizeable population centers, the Great Plains region has few population centers and very few large cities. The Northern Great

Plains Regional Authority is working on a regional transportation plan that will integrate new telecommunications technology and rail, bus, truck, maritime, and air transportation.[61] Certain innovations occurring in air transport may also hold new possibilities for the region in mitigating the impact of remoteness.

In 2001, Congress authorized the Commission on the Future of the U.S. Aerospace Industry (P.L.106-398).[62] The Commission's final report was issued in November, 2002. The report envisions an integrated 21st Century transportation system based on a common infrastructure of communications, navigation, and surveillance systems. The report proposes an "interstate skyway system" — like the Eisenhower highway program of the 1950s and 1960s — using broadband digital communications, precision surveillance and navigation, and high-resolution weather forecasts. Such a system could link small, remote areas within a larger region and thus make them more appealing areas for economic development.

The Commission report reviewed data that suggest the hub-and-spoke system characterizing the existing passenger airline system may become obsolete as it becomes increasingly congested. In its stead, the Commission recommended the further investigation of a Small Aircraft Transport System (SATS), essentially an air-taxi system. Such a system could link small, remote areas within a larger region, and, with capacity for regional travel, some of the disadvantages of remote locations might be mitigated. Whether this innovation could make the Great Plains more attractive to manufacturers is unknown.

The SATS concept is based on a new generation of affordable small aircraft supported by an airborne "internet." Each would operate within a system of small airports serving thousands of suburban, rural and remote communities. The SATS concept makes greater use of small aircraft for personal and business transportation. SATS should be able to do this by increasing the supply of smaller aircraft for "flight-on-demand" and for use in "point-to-point" direct travel between smaller aviation facilities (such as regional airports, general aviation and other landing facilities including heliports).

The SATS architecture would incorporate an advanced, on-board weather data collection system for any landing facility in the United States. SATS would use Internet communications technologies for travel planning and scheduling. SATS research is intended to create the possibility of using landing facilities that would not require control towers or radar surveillance. The SATS architecture would be created to operate within the National Airspace System (NAS), but in a more automated manner among the 5,000 or so existing public-use landing facilities. With a total of over 18,000 of these smaller landing facilities serving vast numbers of communities in the United States, ultimately, all of these facilities could employ SATS operating capabilities.

National Aeronautical and Space Administration (NASA) investments in technologies have led to the emergence of a new generation of small aircraft. These new aircraft would possess near-all-weather operating capabilities and would be compatible with the modernization of the National Airspace System. The new aircraft would incorporate state-of-the-art advancements in avionics, airframes, engines, and advanced pilot training technologies.

Regional Approaches to Rural Economic Development

Introduction

Regional economic development alliances are enjoying a resurgence of interest in many parts of the United States. While the concept of such alliances is not new, its application to rural areas has been minimal. Proponents of regional approaches share the view that the historic pattern of community-based economic development no longer addresses the complexity of rural issues that may characterize a larger geography. The fiscal crises in many states are also creating pressures on many rural communities to seek new solutions to providing essential community services through pooling resources. Largely the creation of state and regional development entities and metropolitan planning organizations, these new regional organizations have adopted two general categories of strategies. First, strategies based on the types of regions involved, i.e., regional organizations that attempt to address common problems arising between urban and rural areas or that better balance urban and rural needs as these areas overlap. A second development category is based on the types of projects in which regions are involved, e.g., building or revitalizing rural cultures, developing broadband capacity, preserving natural resources, enhancing transportation infrastructure.[63]

Congress has had a long history of support for regional authorities such as the Tennessee Valley Authority (TVA) and the Appalachian Regional Commission (ARC). Both the TVA and the ARC have continued to support economic development and social change in their respective regions. A substantial body of literature now exists on the impact of these regional authorities. While there continue to be differences in opinion about the development successes of these authorities, an empirical assessment of ARC's impact over 26 years in the region's 391 counties, concluded that the programs did produce significant growth. Using a methodology based on paired communities, the authors concluded that growth was significantly faster in the 391 Appalachian counties than it was in the control counties. This also held true for Central Appalachia, the poorest sub-region in the ARC. Another reported result was improved local planning in ARC counties compared to the control counties.[64]

More recently, Congress has authorized new regional approaches to common concerns by establishing the Denali Commission (1998), the Delta Regional Authority (2000) and, most recently, the Northern Great Plains Regional Authority (2002). Legislation for three other regional bodies was also introduced in the 108th Congress: (1) a bill to establish a Southwest Border Authority to promote economic development in the border regions of Arizona, California, New Mexico and Texas (S. 458/H.R. 1071); (2) a bill to create a regional authority in the Southeast (H.R. 141), The Southeast Crescent Authority (SECA). The SECA would assist economically distressed communities in Alabama, Georgia, Florida, Mississippi, North Carolina, South Carolina, and Virginia; and (3) a bill to create the Delta Black Belt Regional Authority (H.R. 678). The bill to create the Southwest Border Authority was referred to the Committee on Environment and Public Works in February 2003. The bill to establish the SECA was referred in January, 2003 to the Subcommittee on Economic Development, Public Buildings and Emergency Management of the House Transportation and Infrastructure Committee and in February, 2003 to the Subcommittee on Domestic and International Monetary Policy, Trade, and Technology of the House Financial Services Committee. In June, 2003, the Subcommittee on Economic Development, Public Buildings and Emergency Management forwarded the measure to its Full Committee. The bill to create the Delta Black Belt Regional Authority was referred to the Subcommittee on Domestic and International Monetary Policy, Trade, and Technology on March 10, 2003.

The Northern Great Plains Regional Authority (NGPRA)

The NGPRA is a newly created federal-state-provincial partnership that includes Iowa, Minnesota, Nebraska, North and South Dakota, and the Provinces of Manitoba and Saskatchewan. In 1994, Congress passed the Northern Great Plains Rural Development Act (P.L.103-318). The following year, the Northern Great Plains Rural Development Commission was established. In 1997, the Commission issued its regional development report to Congress and the Commission was sunset. Later that year, NGP, Inc. was established to implement the Commission's recommendations. Discussions with the region's congressional delegation led to a plan to create a regional development authority similar to the one Congress created for the Delta Authority. The Farm Security and Rural Investment Act of 2002 (P.L.107-171, Section 6028) established the NGPRA to implement the Commission's plan and authorized $30 million to be appropriated each year (2002-2007) to support the Authority's programs. No funding, however, was appropriated for the Authority in FY2002 or FY2003. For FY2004, the Authority was provided $1.5 million in funding by the Consolidated Appropriations Act of 2004 (P.L.108-199).

At the local level, the NGPRA intends to rely on the existing network of the Economic Development Administration's (EDA) designated economic development districts to coordinate efforts within a multi-county area. These EDA districts, known as local development districts (LDDs), are regional entities with extensive experience in assisting small municipalities and counties improve basic infrastructure and help stimulate economic growth. They also serve as the delivery mechanism for a variety of other federal and state programs, such as aging, economic development, emergency management, small business development, telecommunications, transportation and workforce development programs.

NGPRA Economic Development Strategies

The NGPRA has identified four areas for their strategic planning: (1) Agriculture and Natural Resources, (2) Economic and Policy Analysis, (3) Information Technology, and (4) Leadership Capacity Development. Given the central role of agriculture in the regional economy, the Authority is integrating into its planning: shifts in consumer demand toward organic foods; a recognition of the shift to supply-chains in production (discussed above) and the corresponding need to develop identity preserved commodities; and the emerging importance of non-food commodities, i.e., bio-based industrial commodities. A central objective is to turn the Great Plains into an internationally recognized center for biomass research and use. These agricultural plans are also grounded more broadly in transforming the transportation systems of the regions, developing local and regional leadership capacity, and expanding the availability and use of information technologies within the region.

Legislation in the 108th Congress

As with past congresses, Members of the 108th Congress have introduced a wide range of bills that would have direct implications for rural areas. Legislation addressing health care, business development, Medicare, community development organizations, telecommunications, transportation, conservation, and Native American issues, among others, either target rural areas specifically or are open to all political jurisdictions. In addition to these initiatives, funds for rural development programs authorized by the 2002 farm bill (P.L.107-171) also provide loan and grant support specifically to rural areas for water and waste water facilities, value-added agricultural development, telemedicine, rural business development, alternative energy, Native Americans, and rural housing.

Two bills introduced in the 108th Congress (H.R. 2194 and S. 602) and discussed below, specifically target areas that have suffered significant population out-migration over the past 20 years. While not designating remote rural areas *per se*, the bills' provisions may be of particular interest to remote areas. Approximately one-third of the 242 remote counties had the population losses in the last decade alone that qualify for assistance authorized in these two bills (see also Figure 1 above). A third bill (H.R. 137) targets rural job creation and labor training from a regional basis. Supporters say that regional approaches to rural development may hold particular promise through the increased recognition of the significant ties that exist between urban/suburban areas and their outlying rural areas.

New Homestead Act (H.R. 2194 and S. 602)

These identical bills provide financial assistance and incentives designed to stem population out-migration from rural areas. The qualifying criterion is that an individual live in or relocate to a county that is (1) outside a metropolitan statistical area and (2) has suffered a 10% or greater population out-migration over the previous 20 years. Modeling itself on the original Homestead Act of 1862, the bill would provide financial incentives to both individuals and businesses. Provisions include:

I. New Homestead Opportunities

- Student loan repayments: Authorizes the Secretary of Education to pay up to a total of $10,000 over five years to any person who (1) completes either an associate or bachelor degree and (2) resides in a qualifying county and (3) is employed in a qualifying county. These provisions would potentially have the effect of stemming the loss of the most educated ;

- Tax incentives for new home buyers: Provides $5,000 tax credit for the home purchases of individuals who locate in qualified areas for five years (or 10% of purchase price, whichever is lower);

- Tax deductions: Protects home values by allowing losses in home value to be deducted from federal income taxes;

- Individual Homestead Accounts: Creates tax-favored accounts to help build savings and increase access to credit. Individuals can contribute a maximum of $2,500 per year for up to five years and there is a government-matching contribution of 25-100% depending on income. Tax and penalty-free distributions can be made after five years for small business loans, education expenses, first-time home purchases, and un-reimbursed medical expenses. Accounts can grow tax-free and all funds are available for withdrawal upon retirement.

II. New Incentives for Main Street Businesses

- Creates Rural Investment Tax Credits to target investments in high out-migration counties. States receive $1 million of these credits per eligible county. Credits are allocated to businesses that move to or expand to a qualifying county. Businesses use these credits to offset the cost of newly constructed or existing buildings. Over a 10-year period, businesses can use these credits to reduce their taxes by as much as 80% of their total investment.

- Authorizes Micro-enterprise Tax Credits to aid small businesses (5 or fewer employees) in high out-migration counties. Micro-enterprises can use the tax credits to reduce their taxes by 30-percent of their qualifying new investment (limited to $25,000 lifetime). For equipment purchases tied to Rural Investment Tax Credit projects, businesses would be able to accelerate the equipment's depreciation.

III. New Homestead Venture Capital Fund

- Establishes a $3 billion venture capital fund to invest in businesses in high out-migration counties. The fund would guarantee up to 40% of private investments in existing business

and start-ups, and up to 60% of such investments in manufacturing or high-technology ventures;
- The fund can take equity positions and extend credit to other approved entities;
- Federal government would invest $200 million per year for 10 years; states and private investors would be required to provide yearly matching funds of $50 million each (or $1 for each $4 of federal funds).

New Homestead Economic Opportunity Act (H.R. 1686)

This bill is almost identical to H.R. 2194 and S. 602. It includes the same titles and authorizes the same provisions with some slight modification (e.g., the student loan repayment maximum is $3000 per year rather than $2000). As with the New Homestead Act, this bill also makes living and working in a county with a 10% population out-migration over the previous 20 years the qualifying criterion for assistance.

Rural America Job Assistance and Creation Act (H.R. 137)

This bill is also aimed at improving the opportunities available to areas where population out-migration is significant.

- Expands the Work Opportunity Tax Credit within designated "development zones" where population has declined, where job growth is low, and where poverty is high;
- Provides grants to business consortia for developing the work skills of regional workers. The training is directed toward the development of skills that are benchmarked to advanced industry practices;
- Provides grants for business "incubators" for newly established small and medium-sized businesses.

Status of Legislation

In June 2003, H.R. 2194 was referred to the House Agriculture Subcommittee on Conservation, Credit, Rural Development and Research and S. 602 was read twice and referred to the Committee on Finance. H.R. 1686 was also referred to the House Agriculture Subcommittee on Conservation, Credit, Rural Development and Research. H.R. 137 was referred to the House Financial Services Committee Subcommittee on Domestic and International Monetary Policy, Trade, and Technology in February, 2003.

CONCLUSION

Some might argue that what is occurring in the remote counties of the Great Plains region today is the inevitable logic of technological progress, the decline of older industries, and the existence of more attractive opportunities in urban areas. Moreover, it represents a long-standing cycle of economic ups and downs for the region. But an argument can also be made that the output-enhancing technologies of public agriculture research were never neutral. From this perspective, it is necessary to review real, tangible costs as well as gains. There is ample evidence that relocation decisions are not uni-dimensional: People do not relocate simply to increase income; opportunities to increase household income are weighed against competing desires and interests. The desire to live in a rural community where one's family has long resided are understandable decisions made with conscious trade-offs. People do leave areas, however, when there are very few choices for gaining a livelihood. Data discussed above indicates that the Great Plains remains disproportionately farm-dependent, that it is suffering a substantial population out-migration, that traditional rural economic development strategies have not been notably successful in the region, and that the Great Plains relies heavily on various forms of federal payments. While such payments also go to other areas in the United States, they are now central to the well-being of many residents of the Great Plains. Yet, the form of payments, i.e., income supports, may not have the same long-term impact as capital investment funds. In the absence of successful efforts to reverse the decline, the result of these various trend lines appears somewhat pessimistic.

Historical evidence reveals how the changing organization of industrial production produces clear winners and clear losers. The rise of the textile industry in 18th century Britain depopulated rural areas in the course of two generations, displaced skilled craftsmen, and forever altered the social and spatial histories of that country. The long trend-line of a shrinking farm sector in the United States is not news. It has happened in every region of the country. But, the conditions in the remote counties of the Great Plains are different in degree if not kind and may require different responses. The slow decline of agricultural employment has not been accompanied by significant opportunities in other areas. One observer testified before Congress, "the farm and ranch communities of the nation's heartland are in the midst of an opportunity crisis."[65]

Some analysts and observers would hold that, in the absence of evidence that public intervention was a necessary correction to otherwise well-functioning markets, what is occurring in the Great Plains, while disruptive, may be inevitable. From that perspective, the question asked above of "Why invest in rural America?" will have been definitively answered by market logic.[66] Not doing anything but allowing existing trends to continue unabated, may, in effect, be a public policy. The consequences of such policy a decision may not have been adequately assessed, however. The great difficulty is determining what the realistic options are from a public policy perspective. Initial congressional efforts to create new incentives to reverse regional population out-migration would predictably be welcomed by Great Plains communities. In their view, reversing population out-migration may be the first order of business.[67]

It can be argued that the Great Plains is not remote because it is economically undeveloped; it is economically undeveloped because it is remote and remains largely dependent on a single dominant but declining economic sector. New initiatives in regional transportation and developments in broadband telecommunications may offer important if partial solutions to some of the problems of remoteness. At their height in the 1960s and 1970s, however, U.S. regional policies to address rural-urban disparities were still relatively modest efforts.[68] Current congressional efforts to expand on regional solutions in other geographic areas may produce outcomes that the Great Plains Regional Authority can adapt to their own circumstances. But unless the areas become more attractive for people to live and work, such interventions may produce only modest changes.[69] Market changes and the deepening of economic internationalization may direct precisely that outcome. Yet, policymakers, rural researchers, and rural observers have yet to fully understand how spatial and socioeconomic environments have interacted to produce the existing development patterns in the Great Plains and retarded alternative patterns.[70] Remoteness is not the only variable in these interactions, but it may serve as a proxy for a multi-dimensional set of characteristics that exerts a powerful influence on the possibilities available to the Great Plains region. Rural development programs that are *place-specific*, i.e., that take existing social and economic development programs and modify them to address the particular circumstances of specific rural areas, could have value to the Great Plains region and other distinctive rural areas.

APPENDIX A. MEASURING RURALITY

Rural development researchers have pointed out the importance of developing more analytically sound rural taxonomies for public policy.[71]

Probably the most widely cited rural typologies were developed by USDA's Economic Research Service These typologies are based on a county's general economic specialization and its policy type (Tables 7 and 8). While they have been very useful for breaking down the great diversity of rural areas into more manageable units, they may not be as useful for targeting rural development policies as typologies that are comprised of multi-dimensional scales. Linking a particular set of rural development policies to varied rural conditions would be aided by the development of a rural taxonomy permitting the delineation of one group of rural places from another based on a set of particular characteristics of the rural places. Remote rural areas have characteristics that are different from, for example, rural areas that are within closer commuting distance to a city. They do not differ from other rural areas simply in terms of their remoteness, although this is a significant characteristic. Rather, remoteness seems to be a central identifier encompassing multidimensional attributes of these areas, for example, significant population loss, low-wages, above average poverty, distinctive demographic characteristics, single-sector economies and/or high-unemployment. Particular combinations of socioeconomic characteristics could be helpful in identifying particular policy regimes to address the particular needs of these areas.[72]

Table 7. USDA Classification of Non-Metro Counties by Economic Type

Economic Type (1)	Definition	Number of Counties (1989 data)
Farming-dependent	Greater than or equal to 20% of total labor and proprietors' income from agriculture	556[73]
Manufacturing-dependent	Greater than or equal to 30% of total income from manufacturing	506
Mining-dependent	Greater than or equal to 20% of total income from mining	146
Government-dependent	Greater than or equal to 25% of total income from government	244
Service-dependent	50% or more of total income from service sector employment (2)	323

Source: Cook, Peggy J. and Karen L. Mizer. *The Revised ERS County Typology.* USDA-ERS, November. 1994.

(1) Economic and policy types can and do overlap

(2) The service sector encompasses a wide variety of employment and includes such areas as areas as retail, business and professional services, education, finance, insurance, and real estate.

Table 8. USDA Classification of Non-Metro Counties by Policy Type

Policy Type (1)	Definition	Number of Counties (1989 data)
Transfer-dependent	25% or more of personal income from Federal/State/local transfer payments (weighted average)	381
Retirement-destination	Population aged 60 and older increased 15% or more during 1980-1990	190
Persistent Poverty	20% or more of county population in each of four years: 1960, 1970, 1980, 1990 with poverty-level income	535
Commuting	40% or more of county's workers commuting outside their county of residence in 1990	381
Federal Lands	30% of county's land area federally owned in 1987	270

Source: Cook, Peggy J. and Karen L. Mizer. *The Revised ERS County Typology.* USDA-ERS, November. 1994.
(1) Economic and policy types can and do overlap.

Researchers at the USDA's Economic Research Service also developed two widely used, unidimensional scales that divide the 3,141 counties, county equivalents, and cities into nine codes. The first (Table 9) classifies urban counties by size and non-metro counties by their degree of urbanization and proximity to a metro area. The scale permits analysis of trends in non-metro areas that may be related to population density and the influences from the metro area. "Adjacent" non-metro counties are physically adjacent to one or more of the Office of Management and Budget's (OMB) Metropolitan Statistical Areas (MSA) *and* have at least 2% of the employed labor force in the non-metro county commuting to cental metro counties. Non-metro counties that do not meet these criteria are classified as "not adjacent."

Table 9. Rural-Urban Continuum Codes

Code	Description
Metropolitan Counties	
1	Counties in metro areas of 1 million population or more
2	Counties in metro areas of 250,000 to 1 million population
3	Counties in metro areas of fewer than 250,000 population
Non-Metropolitan Counties	
4	Urban population of 20,000 or more, adjacent to a metro area
5	Urban population of 20,000 or more, not adjacent to a metro area
6	Urban population of 2,500 to 19,999, adjacent to a metro area.
7	Urban population of 2,500 to 19,999, not adjacent to a metro area
8	Completely rural or less than 2,500 urban population, adjacent to a metro area.
9	Completely rural or less than 2,500 urban population, not adjacent to a metro area.

Source: USDA Economic Research Service.

Table 10 presents a second scale based on the evidence that an area's geographic context has a significant effect on its development. It is somewhat discouraging for rural development researchers to acknowledge that over the past 20 years, most successful rural areas became so through some urban-based influence.[74] The Urban Influence Codes in Table 10 recognize this empirical reality and classify counties both by size and by access to larger economies. Small rural economies with access to centers of trade, finance, and communication fare much better socially and economically than remote counties. While the Internet may make some physical access less important in the future, those rural areas with access to dynamic population centers are more likely than remote rural areas to create and maintain diverse and successful economies.

Table 10. Urban Influence Codes

Code	Description
Metropolitan Counties	
1	Large - in a metro area of 1 million or more population.
2	Small - in a metro area of fewer than 1 million population.
Non-Metropolitan Counties	
3	Adjacent to a large metro area and contains a city of at least 10,000 population.
4	Adjacent to a large metro area and does not contain a city of at least 10,000 population.
5	Adjacent to a small metro area and contains a city of at least 10,000 population.
6	Adjacent to a small metro area and does not contain a city of at least 10,000 population.
7	Not adjacent to a metro area and contains a city of at least 10,000 population.
8	Not adjacent to a metro area and contains a town of at least 2,500-9,999 population.
9	Not adjacent to a metro area and does not contain a city of at least 2,500 population.

Source: USDA Economic Research Service.

The Urban Influence Codes are based on the official OMB metro status as announced in June, 1993, and rely on population and commuting data from the 1990 Census of Population. Non-metro counties are considered adjacent if they abut a metro area and have at least 2% of employed persons commuting to work in a core county of the metropolitan area.

There are 836 metro counties, of which 311 are part of large metro areas and 525 are part of small metro areas. There are 2,305 non-metro counties, 186 adjacent to large metro areas and 63 that contain their own city. Another 815 non-metro counties are adjacent to small metro areas, of which 188 have their own city. Of the 1,304 non-metro counties that are not adjacent to a metro area, 234 have their own city, 555 have a town, and 515 are rural. Not all metro areas are completely surrounded by adjacent counties. Some counties abutting metro areas do not meet the 2% commuting requirement to considered "adjacent." Some of the urban influence groups are concentrated in particular census divisions. The most concentrated are the rural non-adjacent counties: 41% are in the West North Central Division of the United States which includes Nebraska, South Dakota, North Dakota, and Montana.

Appendix B. Top 25 Industries in Low-Wage Rural Counties

Rank	Standard Industrial Classification	Low-Wage Counties			Other Rural Counties	
		Share of Jobs (%)	Annual Earnings per Job	Rank	Share of Jobs (%)	Annual Earnings per Job
1	Elementary and secondary schools	10.6	$20,230	1	7.5	$22,487
2	Eating/drinking places	7.3	$6,997	2	6.6	$7,788
3	Grocery stores	4.1	$10,671	4	3.4	$12,047
4	Nursing and personal care	3.9	$12,015	5	2.4	$13,981
5	Government offices	3.5	$14,062	7	2.0	$18,572
6	Hospitals	3.4	$19,917	3	3.9	$24,161
7	Hotels and motels	2.2	$9,878	9	1.6	$12,584
8	Mens/boys clothing	2.1	$12,714	25	0.7	$14,705
9	Banks	2.0	$22,291	12	1.3	$23,091
10	Amusement/recreation	1.5	$12,611	14	1.1	$13,498
11	Gas stations	1.5	$10,674	17	1.0	$11,907
12	Trucking and courier	1.4	$21,067	10	1.6	$24,714
13	Meatpacking	1.4	$15,817	11	1.4	$19,986
14	Department stores	1.3	$11,352	6	2.0	$12,216
15	Public safety	1.0	$20,289	13	1.3	$27,359
16	Solid waste management	0.9	$24,682	44	0.5	$28,274
17	Sawmills	0.9	$18,725	22	0.7	$24,311
18	U.S. Postal Service	0.9	$26,783	28	0.6	$30,625
19	Medical offices/clinics	0.9	$30,364	15	1.1	$42,290

Appendix B. (Continued)

20	**Farm wholesaling**	0.9	$15,044	64	0.3	$18,758		
21	Car dealers	0.9	$23,171	18	0.9	$27,269		
22	**Family services**	0.9	$13,499	24	0.7	$15,386		
23	Home health care	0.8	$16,458	40	0.6	$16,678		
24	Nondurable wholesaling	0.8	$19,581	31	0.6	$21,533		
25	Highway construction	0.8	$20,963	29	0.6	$21,147		

Source: 1995 Bureau of Labor Statistical data prepared by USDA Economic Research Service (Gibbs and Cromartie at footnote 39, above).

Note: Industries with average earning per job in low-wage counties below the four-person poverty threshold are in bold.

The following tables in Appendices C-I present socioeconomic data on the 242 remote rural counties in seven states of the Great Plains region. Two criteria were used to select the counties: (1) a county population density of 6 or fewer persons per square mile and (2) a Rural-Urban Continuum Code of 6-9 and a Urban Influence Code of 6-9. Only a few of these counties have codes less than 8, making them among the most rural counties in the United States. For a description of these two scales, see Appendix A above.

These county codes are based on the 1990 Census data on worker commuting and the 1993 classification of OMB Metropolitan Statistical Areas (MSA). New Urban Influence Codes and new Rural-Urban Continuum Codes based on the 2000 Census are not expected to be available until mid-2004. The development of updated codes requires commuting data (journey-to-work) from the U.S. Census and the new updated OMB Metropolitan Statistical Areas.

APPENDIX C. REMOTE KANSAS COUNTIES

Table 1

Kansas Counties	Rural-Urban Continuum Code	Urban Influence Code	Population, 2000	Population Change, 1990–2000 (%) (Negative numbers in parentheses)	Population Density (pop/sq.mi.)	Median Household Income ($) 2000	Poverty Rate (%)	Unemployment Rate, 2001 (%)	Average wage per non-farm job, 2000
Barber	9	9	5307	(10)	5.2	$33,407	10.1	3.3	$19,725
Chase	9	9	3030	0	3.9	$32,656	8.6	4.3	$17,386
Clark	9	9	2390	(1)	3.2	$33,857	12.7	1.7	$21,111
Comanche	9	9	1967	(15)	2.9	$29,415	10.2	1.5	$15,604
Decatur	9	9	3472	(14)	4.5	$30,257	11.6	2.3	$15,502
Elk	9	9	3261	2	5.1	$27,267	13.8	4.9	$16,702
Gove	9	9	3068	5	5.1	$33,510	10.3	1.6	$18,690
Graham	8	6	2946	(17)	3.0	$31,286	11.5	2.3	$18,616
Greeley	9	9	1534	(13.5)	3.9	$34,605	11.6	3.6	$19,158
Hamilton	9	9	2670	11.8	2.4	$32,033	11.5	1.8	$20,354
Hodgeman	9	9	2085	(4.2)	2.5	$35,994	11.5	2.7	$18,900
Jewell	9	9	3791	(10.8)	4.7	$30,537	11.6	1.7	$16,557
Kearny	9	9	4531	12.5	4.6	$40,149	11.7	4.5	$20,742
Kiowa	9	9	3278	(10.4)	5.1	$31,576	10.8	2.1	$18,275
Lane	9	9	2155	(9.3)	3.3	$36,047	8.2	3.9	$20,761
Lincoln	9	9	3578	(2.1)	5.1	$30,893	9.7	2.9	$16,288
Logan	9	9	3046	(1.1)	2.9	$32,131	7.3	2.5	$19,534
Meade	9	9	4631	9.0	4.3	$36,761	9.3	2.1	$21,862

Table 1 (Continued)

Kansas Counties	Rural-Urban Continuum Code	Urban Influence Code	Population, 2000	Population Change, 1990-2000 (%) (Negative numbers in parentheses)	Population Density (pop/sq.mi.)	Median Household Income ($) 2000	Poverty Rate (%)	Unemployment Rate, 2001 (%)	Average wage per non-farm job, 2000
Morton	9	9	3496	0.5	4.8	$37,232	10.5	2.4	$26,057
Ness	9	9	3454	(14.4)	3.8	$32,340	8.7	1.8	$19,575
Osborne	9	9	4452	(8.5)	5.5	$29,145	10.4	3.1	$16,730
Rawlins	9	9	2966	(12.9)	3.2	$32,105	12.5	2.5	$17,961
Rush	9	9	3551	(7.6)	5.3	$31,268	9.7	2.3	$21,042
Sheridan	9	9	2813	(7.6)	3.4	$33,547	15.7	1.7	$21,394
Smith	9	9	4536	(10.7)	5.7	$28,486	10.7	1.9	$17,458
Stanton	9	9	2406	3.1	3.4	$40,172	14.9	2.1	$20,759
Trego	9	9	3319	(10.2)	4.2	$29,677	12.3	2.2	$17,719
Wallace	9	9	1749	(4.0)	2.0	$33,000	16.1	3.0	$17,236
Wichita	9	9	2531	(8.2)	3.8	$33,462	14.8	3.2	$22,029
County Average			3173	(5.1)	4.0	$32,856	11.3	2.6	$19,094
Kansas			2.69 million	8.5	32.9	$40,624	9.9	4.3	$29,360
United States			281.4 million	13.1	79.6	$41,994	12.4	4.8	$35,323

Table 2

Kansas Counties	Population, 2000	Population, 65 and older (%)	High-School graduates, 25 and older (%)	Bachelors degree or higher, (%)	Private non-farm employment change, 1990-1999 (Negative numbers in parentheses)	Per capita income change, 1990-2000 (Negative numbers in parentheses)	Per capita income change, 1980-2000 (Negative numbers in parentheses)
Barber	5307	21.5	85.8	21.0	2.4	0.2	(8.8)
Chase	3030	18.7	87.1	19.6	(42.5)	26.6	20.6
Clark	2390	21.8	87.4	22.1	27.4	(14.9)	12.4
Comanche	1967	25.8	91.3	15.1	3.8	(20.5)	22.3
Decatur	3472	26.2	86.4	15.4	(16.2)	(3.0)	10.5
Elk	3261	25.3	80.0	10.6	5.2	9.2	17.5
Gove	3068	22.7	84.5	18.4	28.3	(23.6)	47.8
Graham	2946	23.7	83.6	17.4	23.0	16.7	53.2
Greeley	1534	17.7	83.7	17.4	(0.9)	(19.9)	13.4
Hamilton	2670	18.4	76.7	17.4	73.1	(10.6)	48.8
Hodgeman	2085	19.0	86.9	19.7	128.3	(3.0)	63.6
Jewell	3791	25.9	87.6	13.8	22.1	(13.7)	38.7
Kearny	4531	11.1	75.8	15.0	58.7	(29.2)	34.3
Kiowa	3278	21.3	85.2	18.9	26.7	(1.1)	32.9

Table 2 (Continued)

Kansas Counties	Population, 2000	Population 65 and older (%)	High-School graduates, 25 and older (%)	Bachelors degree or higher, (%)	Private non-farm employment change, 1990-1999 (Negative numbers in parentheses)	Per capita income change, 1990-2000 (Negative numbers in parentheses)	Per capita income change, 1980-2000 (Negative numbers in parentheses)
Lane	2155	20.5	88.5	18.5	27.0	(4.6)	15.1
Lincoln	3578	23.5	85.0	17.4	97.1	(6.8)	3.7
Logan	3046	20.7	86.7	17.5	14.7	(9.3)	(5.0)
Meade	4631	17.9	80.3	19.6	56.4	6.9	36.0
Morton	3496	13.9	81.9	16.6	72.4	15.2	29.2
Ness	3454	24.2	84.4	17.9	36.6	(2.4)	18.5
Osborne	4452	25.7	84.8	15.5	7.6	(9.5)	17.9
Rawlins	2966	25.6	84.7	15.9	19.2	(3.1)	35.9
Rush	3551	25.3	82.8	16.4	31.6	0.4	(0.3)
Sheridan	2813	20.3	87.8	15.9	28.6	14.2	64.3
Smith	4536	27.9	84.6	16.7	6.7	7.7	32.6
Stanton	2406	13.0	78.0	16.9	52.7	(20.2)	62.3
Trego	3319	24.0	84.3	14.0	15.7	(8.6)	7.3
Wallace	1749	18.1	84.0	17.2	41.8	2.0	22.6

Table 2 (Continued)

Kansas Counties	Population, 2000	Population, 65 and older (%)	High-School graduates, 25 and older (%)	Bachelors degree or higher, (%)	Private non-farm employment change, 1990-1999 (Negative numbers in parentheses)	Per capita income change, 1990-2000 (Negative numbers in parentheses)	Per capita income change, 1980-2000 (Negative numbers in parentheses)
Wichita	2531	16.0	77.7	15.5	56.2	(28.5)	60.2
County Average	3173	21.2	84.1	17.0	31.2	(4.6)	27.8
Kansas	2.69 million	13.3	86.0	25.8	18.4	14.3	30.5
United States	281.4	12.4	80.4	24.4	18.4	21.3	65.4

Sources: U.S. Department of Commerce, Bureau of the Census; U.S. Department of Labor, Bureau of Labor Statistics; USDA, Economic Research Service; U.S. Department of Commerce, Bureau of Economic Analysis.

APPENDIX D. REMOTE MONTANA COUNTIES

Table 1

Montana Counties	Rural-Urban Continuum Code	Urban Influence Code	Population, 2000	Population Change, 1990-2000 (%) (Negative numbers in parentheses)	Population Density (pop/sq.mi.)	Median Household Income ($) 2000	Poverty Rate (%)	Unemployment Rate, 2001 (%)	Average wage per non-farm job 2000
Beaverhead	7	8	9202	9.2	1.5	$28,962	17.1	3.3	$21,025
Bighorn	6	6	12671	11.8	2.3	$27,684	29.2	16.8	$24,234
Blaine	9	9	7009	4.2	1.6	$25,247	28.1	5.6	$20,516
Broadwater	9	9	4385	32.2	2.8	$32,689	10.8	4.3	$23,852
Carbon	8	6	9552	18.2	3.9	$32,139	11.6	4.6	$17,971
Carter	9	9	1360	(9.5)	0.5	$26,312	18.1	2.3	$14,572
Chouteau	8	6	5970	9.5	1.4	$29,150	20.5	3.1	$16,823
Custer	7	8	11696	0.0	3.1	$30,000	15.1	3.7	$21,695
Daniels	9	9	2017	(11.0)	1.6	$27,306	16.9	2.8	$20,597
Dawson	7	8	9059	(4.7)	4	$31,393	14.9	2.7	$19,602
Fallon	9	9	2837	(8.6)	1.9	$29,944	12.5	2.6	$22,622
Fergus	7	8	11893	(1.6)	2.8	$30,409	15.4	5.8	$20,657

Table 1 (Continued)

Montana Counties	Rural-Urban Continuum Code	Urban Influence Code	Population, 2000	Population Change, 1990-2000 (%) (Negative numbers in parentheses)	Population Density (pop/sq.mi.)	Median Household Income ($) 2000	Poverty Rate (%)	Unemployment Rate, 2001 (%)	Average wage per non-farm job 2000
Garfield	9	9	1279	(19.5)	0.3	$25,917	21.5	2.2	$16,007
Glacier	7	8	13247	9.3	4	$27,921	27.3	11.1	$22,496
Golden Valley	8	6	1042	14.3	0.8	$27,308	25.8	4.7	$17,226
Granite	9	9	2830	11.1	1.5	$27,813	16.8	7.7	$19,266
Jefferson	7	7	10049	26.6	4.8	$41,506	9.0	4.4	$25,616
Judith Basin	8	6	2329	2.1	1.2	$29,241	21.1	3.7	$17,933
Liberty	9	9	2158	(6.0)	1.6	$30,284	20.3	2.9	$19,513
Lincoln	7	8	18837	7.8	4.8	$26,754	19.2	11.3	$22,503
Madison	9	9	6851	14.4	1.7	$30,233	12.1	3.4	$19,597
McCone	9	9	1977	(13.1)	0.9	$29,718	16.8	2.3	$19,585
Meagher	8	6	1932	6.2	0.8	$29,375	18.9	5.9	$17,876
Mineral	9	9	3884	17.2	2.7	$27,143	15.8	8.2	$19,074
Mussel Shell	8	6	4497	9.5	2.2	$25,527	19.9	6.6	$17,639

Table 1 (Continued)

Montana Counties	Rural-Urban Continuum Code	Urban Influence Code	Population, 2000	Population Change, 1990-2000 (%) (Negative numbers in parentheses)	Population Density (pop/sq.mi.)	Median Household Income ($) 2000	Poverty Rate (%)	Unemployment Rate, 2001 (%)	Average wage per non-farm job 2000
Park	7	8	15694	8.1	5.5	$31,739	11.4	4.7	$19,412
Petroleum	9	9	493	(5.0)	0.3	$24,107	23.2	2.4	$16,212
Phillips	9	9	4601	(10.9)	1	$28,702	18.3	4.4	$18,769
Pondera	7	8	6424	0.1	4	$30,464	18.8	4.2	$20,180
Powder River	9	9	1858	(11.1)	0.6	$28,398	12.9	1.9	$15,200
Powell	7	8	7180	8.5	2.8	$30,625	12.6	4.8	$23,862
Prairie	9	9	1199	(13.3)	0.8	$25,451	17.2	4.6	$16,765
Richland	7	8	9667	(9.8)	5.1	$32,110	12.2	4.9	$21,219
Roosevelt	7	8	10620	(3.4)	4.7	$24,834	32.4	7.2	$19,971
Rosebud	7	8	9383	(10.7)	2.1	$35,898	22.4	7.1	$29,318
Sanders	9	9	10227	18.0	3.1	$26,852	17.2	8.3	$19,929
Sheridan	9	9	4105	(13.3)	2.8	$29,518	14.7	3.2	$18,185
Still Water	8	6	8195	25.4	3.6	$39,205	9.8	3.1	$37,366

Table 1 (Continued)

Montana Counties	Rural-Urban Continuum Code	Urban Influence Code	Population, 2000	Population Change, 1990-2000, (%) (Negative numbers in parentheses)	Population Density (pop/sq.mi.)	Median Household Income ($) 2000	Poverty Rate (%)	Unemployment Rate, 2001 (%)	Average wage per non-farm job 2000
Sweet Grass	9	9	3609	14.4	1.7	$32,422	11.4	2.6	$18,244
Teton	8	6	6445	2.8	2.8	$30,197	16.6	3.5	$19,512
Toole	7	8	5267	4.4	2.6	$30,169	12.9	2.7	$21,916
Treasure	8	6	861	(1.5)	0.9	$29,830	14.7	3.2	$17,393
Valley	7	8	7675	(6.8)	1.7	$30,979	13.5	3.5	$19,986
Wheatland	9	9	2259	0.6	1.6	$24,492	20.4	3.5	$16,953
Wibaux	9	9	1068	(10.3)	0.2	$28,224	15.3	2.6	$16,109
County Average			6120	2.6	2.3	$29,426	17.4	4.8	$20,111
Montana			902195	12.9	6.2	$33,024	14.6	4.6	$24,274
United States			281.4 million	13.1	79.6	$41,994	12.4	4.8	$35,323

Table 2

Montana Counties	Population, 2000	Population 65 and older	High-School graduates, 25 and older (%)	Bachelors degree or higher, (%)	Private non-farm employment change, 1990-1999	Per capita income change, 1990-2000 (Negative numbers in parentheses)	Per capita income change, 1980-2000
Beaverhead	9202	13.6	89.3	26.4	39.5	8.0	27.5
Big Horn	12671	8.6	76.4	14.3	22.9	3.8	(14.1)
Blaine	7009	12.9	78.7	17.4	3.3	(5.6)	166.3
Broadwater	4385	16.4	85.2	15.0	46.9	6.4	22.2
Carbon	9552	16.8	88.1	23.3	43.2	7.9	20.5
Carter	1360	17.9	83.3	13.6	(15.9)	7.3	16.1
Chouteau	5970	17.5	87.1	20.5	26.4	(32.6)	15.1
Custer	11696	17.1	84.9	18.8	21.8	4.1	(0.4)
Daniels	2017	23.5	85.3	14.1	36.5	37.3	63.4
Dawson	9059	17.7	82.7	15.1	6.6	11.3	(2.4)
Fallon	2837	17.9	85.7	14.4	33.3	13.3	(7.8)
Fergus	11893	19.9	86.3	19.1	18.2	5.7	15.1
Garfield	1279	19.3	84.7	16.8	(6.8)	11.8	23.5

Table 2 (Continued)

Montana Counties	Population, 2000	Population 65 and older	High-School graduates, 25 and older (%)	Bachelors degree or higher, (%)	Private non-farm employment change, 1990-1999	Per capita income change, 1990-2000 (Negative numbers in parentheses)	Per capita income change, 1980-2000
Glacier	13247	9.2	78.6	16.5	9.2	6.1	(21.2)
Golden Valley	1042	16.5	70.5	16.2	43.2	(0.5)	19.2
Granite	2830	15.9	87.8	22.1	18.4	(0.8)	8.4
Jefferson	10049	10.3	90.2	27.7	83.5	10.9	29.6
Judith Basin	2329	17.2	87.6	23.6	(33.0)	(16.1)	26.4
Liberty	2158	19.7	75.0	17.6	59.8	(26.2)	0.7
Lincoln	18837	15.2	80.2	13.7	(3.9)	0.9	12.7
Madison	6851	17.2	89.8	25.5	7.2	11.7	21.2
McCone	1977	18.9	86.1	16.4	(7.4)	22.2	22.5
Meagher	1932	18.2	83.4	18.7	10.1	2.2	34.5
Mineral	3884	14.2	83.2	12.3	3.7	0.5	3.9
Musselshell	4497	17.5	82.6	16.7	(8.0)	(7.6)	(26.2)
Park	15694	14.9	87.6	23.1	28.2	15.4	6.9
Petroleum	493	17.0	82.9	17.4	(15.4)	(0.1)	117.2

Table 2 (Continued)

Montana Counties	Population, 2000	Population 65 and older	High-School graduates, 25 and older (%)	Bachelors degree or higher, (%)	Private non-farm employment change, 1990-1 999	Per capita income change, 1990-2000 (Negative numbers in parentheses)	Per capita income change, 1980-2000
Phillips	4601	17.6	82.4	17.1	(7.2)	(2.6)	20.8
Pondera	6424	3.0	81.6	19.8	10.6	(4.9)	16.9
Powder River	1858	18.5	83.4	16.0	31.8	1.9	(8.3)
Powell	7180	14.0	81.9	13.1	16.6	5.6	13.4
Prairie	1199	24.1	78.8	14.8	116.7	14.1	26.1
Richland	9667	15.6	83.5	17.2	9.4	16.5	6.8
Roosevelt	10620	11.6	80.6	15.6	(3.2)	24.7	17.3
Rosebud	9383	8.9	84.4	17.6	(8.6)	6.6	28.4
Sanders	10227	16.9	81.2	15.5	27.1	4.5	12.5
Sheridan	4105	23.6	81.2	18.4	6.1	28.5	34.5
Stillwater	8195	14.5	87.5	17.8	7.0	29.4	31.8
Sweet Grass	3609	17.6	88.9	23.6	29.6	1.0	6.3
Teton	6445	16.6	83.4	20.8	34.7	(11.7)	15.7
Toole	5267	15.9	81.0	16.8	20.0	(11.3)	(3.0)

Table 2 (Continued)

Montana Counties	Population, 2000	Population 65 and older	High-School graduates, 25 and older (%)	Bachelors degree or higher, (%)	Private non-farm employment change, 1990-1 999	Per capita income change, 1990-2000 (Negative numbers in parentheses)	Per capita income change, 1980-2000
Treasure	861	16.7	86.3	18.2	(6.7)	(16.0)	(20.9)
Valley	7675	19.0	83.9	15.7	10.4	24.2	37.7
Wheatland	2259	19.3	69.0	13.5	14.7	(14.6)	(6.7)
Wibaux	1068	21.5	76.8	16.0	80.2	13.9	7.8
County Average	902195	16.4	83.1	17.9	19.1	4.6	18.6
Montana	902195	13.4	87.2	24.4	30.0	10.2	17.9
United States	281.4 million	12.4	80.4	24.4	18.4	21.3	65.4

Sources: U.S. Department of Commerce, Bureau of the Census; U.S. Department of Labor, Bureau of Labor Statistics; USDA, Economic Research Service; U.S. Department of Commerce, Bureau of Economic Analysis.

APPENDIX E. REMOTE NEBRASKA COUNTIES

Table 1

Nebraska Counties	Rural-Urban Continuum Code	Urban Influence Code	Population, 2000	1990-2000 (%) (Negative numbers in parentheses)	Population Density (pop/sq.mi.)	Median Household Income ($), 2000	Poverty Rate (%)	Unemployment Rate, 2001 (%)	Average wage per non-farm job, 2000
Arthur	9	9	444	(3.9)	0.6	$27,375	13.8	3.4	$13,194
Banner	9	9	819	(3.9)	1.1	$31,399	13.6	1.7	$18,604
Blaine	9	9	583	(13.6)	0.9	$25,278	19.4	1.6	$19,878
Boyd	9	9	2438	(14.0)	5.2	$26,075	15.2	3.8	$16,518
Brown	9	9	3525	(3.6)	3	$28,356	11.1	3.4	$19,007
Chase	9	9	4068	(7.1)	4.9	$32,551	9.6	2.2	$19,666
Cherry	7	8	6148	(2.5)	1.1	$29,268	12.3	1.8	$17,457
Custer	7	8	11793	(3.9)	4.8	$30,677	12.4	1.9	$20,363
Deuel	9	9	2098	(6.2)	5.1	$32,981	9.1	2.8	$18,206
Dundy	9	9	2292	(11.2)	2.8	$27,010	13.6	2.0	$20,528
Frontier	9	9	3099	(0.1)	3.2	$33,038	12.2	2.1	$19,218
Garden	9	9	2293	(6.8)	1.4	$26,458	14.8	3.1	$20,618

Table 1 (Continued)

Nebraska Counties	Rural-Urban Continuum Code	Urban Influence Code	Population, 2000	1990-2000 (%) (Negative numbers in parentheses)	Population Density (pop/sq.mi.)	Median Household Income ($), 2000	Poverty Rate (%)	Unemployment Rate, 2001 (%)	Average wage per non-farm job, 2000
Garfield	9	9	1902	(11.2)	3.8	$27,407	12.6	1.8	$16,320
Gosper	9	9	2143	11.2	4.2	$36,827	7.9	2.2	$17,688
Grant	9	9	747	(2.9)	1	$34,821	9.7	1.7	$15,951
Greeley	9	9	2714	(9.7)	5.3	$28,375	14.6	3.0	$17,299
Hayes	9	9	1068	(12.6)	1.7	$26,667	18.4	2.4	$18,342
Hitchcock	9	9	3111	(17.0)	5.3	$28,287	14.9	3.1	$18,657
Holt	7	8	11551	(8.3)	5.2	$30,738	13.0	3.0	$18,439
Hooker	9	9	783	(1.3)	1.1	$27,868	6.9	3.1	$14,879
Keya Paha	9	9	983	(4.5)	1.3	$24,911	26.9	1.3	$21,236
Kimball	6	6	4089	(0.5)	4.3	$30,586	11.1	2.2	$18,881
Logan	9	9	774	(11.8)	1.5	$33,125	10.5	2.3	$16,025
Loup	9	9	712	4.2	1.2	$26,250	17.7	1.9	$15,521
McPherson	9	9	533	(2.4)	0.6	$25,750	16.2	1.0	$13,703
Morrill	9	9	5440	0.3	3.8	$30,235	14.7	2.8	$18,879

Table 1 (Continued)

Nebraska Counties	Rural-Urban Continuum Code	Urban Influence Code	Population, 2000	1990-2000 (%) (Negative numbers in parentheses)	Population Density (pop/sq.mi.)	Median Household Income ($), 2000	Poverty Rate (%)	Unemployment Rate, 2001 (%)	Average wage per non-farm job, 2000
Perkins	9	9	3200	(5.0)	3.8	$34,205	13.6	1.9	$20,938
Rock	9	9	1756	(13.0)	2	$25,795	0.0	3.8	$16,753
Sheridan	9	9	6198	(8.2)	2.8	$29,484	13.2	2.7	$16,713
Sioux	9	9	1475	(4.8)	0.7	$29,851	15.4	1.3	$14,792
Thomas	9	9	729	(14.3)	1.2	$27,292	14.3	5.7	$17,865
Wheeler	9	9	886	(6.5)	1.6	$26,771	20.9	2.9	$18,795
County Average			2825	(6.1)	2.7	$29,241	13.4	2.5	$17,842
Nebraska			1.4 million	8.4	22.3	$39,250	9.7	3.1	$27,692
United States			281.4 million	13.1	79.6	$41,994	12.4	4.8	$35,323

Table 2.

Nebraska Counties	Population, 2000	Population 65 and older	High-School graduates, 25 and older (%)	Bachelors degree or higher, (%)	Private non-farm employment change, 1990-1 999	Per capita income change, 1990-2000 (Negative numbers in parentheses)	Per capita income change, 1980-2000 (Negative numbers in parentheses)
Arthur	444	16.4	89.5	15.7	(7.0)	(36.8)	(42.4)
Banner	819	16.0	94.2	19.6	NA	(11.7)	(56.8)
Blaine	583	16.8	93.4	12.3	NA	(43.7)	(12.2)
Boyd	2438	24.3	83.0	12.8	33.1	(13.0)	(12.9)
Brown	3525	22.5	83.3	17.2	25.6	(6.8)	16.3
Chase	4068	21.1	86.4	16.6	26.7	9.5	58.0
Cherry	6148	17.3	85.3	19.4	48.0	1.5	6.3
Custer	11793	21.1	87.5	16.1	2.8	7.6	56.6
Deuel	2098	22.9	85.3	17.4	30.8	(6.7)	(15.3)
Dundy	2292	22.4	82.4	16.7	30.1	4.5	80.3
Frontier	3099	16.9	88.3	17.9	33.2	1.7	57.1
Garden	2293	24.0	85.2	14.2	(0.5)	(2.9)	(16.4)
Garfield	1902	24.8	81.1	13.4	1.2	24.5	65.8
Gosper	2143	20.8	88.9	17.6	7.1	(9.0)	89.7

Table 2

Nebraska Counties	Population, 2000	Population 65 and older	High-School graduates, 25 and older (%)	Bachelors degree or higher, (%)	Private non-farm employment change, 1990-1 999	Per capita income change, 1990-2000 (Negative numbers in parentheses)	Per capita income change, 1980-2000 (Negative numbers in parentheses)
Grant	747	13.7	90.3	24.7	46.8	(19.0)	(27.1)
Greeley	2714	23.2	83.2	13.5	20.0	(7.4)	94.3
Hayes	1068	19.9	89.1	11.6	(5.1)	(37.1)	50.0
Hitchcock	3111	22.3	85.6	13.8	(15.5)	(8.8)	12.8
Holt	11551	19.8	84.5	14.5	19.5	4.7	73.1
Hooker	783	26.9	89.7	15.7	47.9	(25.3)	(12.3)
Keya Paha	983	20.7	82.2	15.7	(21.2)	(17.2)	38.5
Kimball	4089	21.0	84.6	13.5	38.9	0.7	(6.8)
Logan	774	17.6	90.8	10.5	28.9	(10.6)	(9.3)
Loup	712	19.5	91.8	13.3	(36.8)	(47.6)	(49.3)
McPherson	533	18.2	88.6	22.2	(36.4)	(40.3)	(27.5)
Morrill	5440	17.0	79.4	14.3	25.8	(13.4)	(22.1)
Perkins	3200	19.3	87.1	17.6	50.7	(7.1)	(0.7)
Rock	1756	22.3	87.4	12.2	38.5	(18.8)	41.2

Table 2 (Continued)

Nebraska Counties	Population, 2000	Population 65 and older	High-School graduates, 25 and older (%)	Bachelors degree or higher, (%)	Private non-farm employment change, 1990-1999	Per capita income change, 1990-2000 (Negative numbers in parentheses)	Per capita income change, 1980-2000 (Negative numbers in parentheses)
Sheridan	6198	21.7	86.1	17.2	18.6	7.2	6.7
Sioux	1475	16.2	86.4	21.5	(82.1)	(36.6)	(50.2)
Thomas	729	20.3	83.7	17.2	186.4	10.2	(15.8)
Wheeler	886	16.8	90.8	14.9	(31.5)	(7.8)	140.3
County Average	2659	20.1	86.7	16.0	17.5	(11.1)	15.9
Nebraska	1.4 million	13.6	86.6	23.7	25.0	16.0	42.6
United States	281.4 million	12.4	80.4	24.4	18.4	21.3	65.4

Sources: U.S. Department of Commerce, Bureau of the Census; U.S. Department of Labor, Bureau of Labor Statistics; USDA, Economic Research Service; U.S. Department of Commerce, Bureau of Economic Analysis.

APPENDIX F. REMOTE NORTH DAKOTA COUNTIES

Table 1

North Dakota Counties	Rural-Urban Continuum	Urban Influence Code	Population, 2000	1990-2000 (%) (Negative numbers in	Population Density (pop/sq.mi.)	Median Household Income ($), 2000	Poverty Rate (%)	Unemployment Rate, 2001 (%)	Average wage per non-farm job, 2000
Adams	9	9	2593	(18.3)	3.2	$29,079	10.4	2.0	$19,407
Benson	9	9	6964	(3.3)	5.2	$26,668	29.1	7.5	$21,613
Billings	9	9	888	(19.9)	1.0	$32,667	12.8	3.9	$16,890
Bottineau	7	8	7149	(10.8)	4.8	$29,853	10.7	3.1	$19,113
Bowman	9	9	3242	(9.8)	3.1	$31,906	8.2	1.9	$18,126
Burke	9	9	2242	(25.3)	2.7	$25,330	15.4	2.5	$21,444
Cavalier	9	9	4831	(20.3)	4.1	$31,868	11.5	2.9	$20,209
Dickey	9	9	5757	(5.7)	5.4	$29,231	14.8	2.2	$19,293
Divide	9	9	2283	(21.2)	2.3	$30,089	14.6	1.9	$15,699
Dunn	9	9	3600	(10.1)	2.0	$30,015	17.5	3.6	$20,235
Eddy	9	9	2757	(6.6)	4.7	$28,642	9.7	4.8	$18,615
Emmons	8	6	4331	(10.3)	3.2	$26,119	20.1	4.6	$18,149
Golden Valley	9	9	1924	(8.7)	2.1	$29,967	15.3	2.1	$16,948

Table 1 (Continued)

North Dakota Counties	Rural-Urban Continuum	Urban Influence Code	Population, 2000	1990-2000 (%) (Negative numbers in	Population Density (pop/sq.mi.)	Median Household Income ($), 2000	Poverty Rate (%)	Unemployment Rate, 2001 (%)	Average wage per non-farm job, 2000
Grant	8	6	2841	(19.9)	2.1	$23,165	20.3	2.7	$16,760
Griggs	9	9	2754	(16.6)	4.7	$29,572	10.1	1.7	$20,207
Hettinger	9	9	2715	(21.2)	3.0	$29,209	14.8	2.2	$18,839
Kidder	9	9	2753	(17.4)	2.5	$25,389	19.8	5.3	$17,760
La Moure	9	9	4701	(12.7)	4.7	$29,707	14.7	2.9	$18,000
Logan	9	9	2308	(18.9)	2.9	$27,986	15.1	2.2	$16,140
McHenry	9	9	5987	(8.3)	3.5	$27,274	15.8	5.0	$19,036
McIntosh	9	9	3390	(15.7)	4.1	$26,389	15.4	2.2	$16,826
McKenzie	9	9	5737	(10.1)	2.3	$29,342	17.2	2.6	$22,896
McLean	8	6	9311	(11.0)	5.0	$32,337	13.5	5.9	$25,880
Mountrail	9	9	6631	(5.6)	3.8	$27,098	19.3	4.7	$20,791
Nelson	8	6	3715	(15.8)	4.5	$28,892	10.3	4.0	$17,154
Oliver	8	6	2065	(13.3)	3.3	$36,650	14.9	4.9	$42,407
Pierce	7	8	4675	(7.5)	5.0	$26,524	12.5	3.3	$18,035
Renville	9	9	2610	(17.4)	3.6	$30,746	11	1.9	$19,179

Table 1 (Continued)

North Dakota Counties	Rural-Urban Continuum	Urban Influence Code	Population, 2000	1990-2000 (%) (Negative numbers in	Population Density (pop/sq.mi.)	Median Household Income ($), 2000	Poverty Rate (%)	Unemployment Rate, 2001 (%)	Average wage per non-farm job, 2000
Sargent	9	9	4366	(4.0)	5.3	$37,213	8.2	2.8	$33,929
Sheridan	9	9	1710	(20.4)	2.2	$24,450	21	6.2	$18,693
Sioux	9	9	4044	7.5	3.4	$22,483	39.2	5.4	$24,520
Slope	9	9	767	(15.4)	0.7	$24,667	16.9	2.2	$10,375
Steele	8	6	2258	(6.7)	3.4	$35,757	7.1	1.2	$22,101
Towner	9	9	2876	(20.7)	3.5	$32,740	8.9	2.7	$19,638
Wells	9	9	5102	(13.0)	4.6	$31,894	13.5	3.4	$17,796
County Average			3768	(13.0)	3.5	$29,169	15	3.4	$20,077
North Dakota			642200	(1.2)	9.3	$34,604	11.9	2.8	$24,683
United States			281.4 million	13.1	79.6	$41,994	12.4	4.8	$35,323

Table 2.

North Dakota Counties	Population, 2000	Population 65 and older	High-School graduates, 25 and older (%)	Bachelors degree or higher, (%)	Private non-farm employment change, 1990-1999	Per capita income change, 1990-2000 (Negative numbers in parentheses)	Per capita income change, 1980-2000 (Negative numbers in parentheses)
Adams	2593	24.1	83.1	16.6	(4.5)	24.1	48.9
Benson	6964	13.5	73.8	10.9	18.6	(10.6)	47.0
Billings	888	13.5	77.8	18.8	66.3	23.9	(2.8)
Bottineau	7149	21.3	81.3	14.9	21.5	15.2	75.9
Bowman	3242	21.8	82.2	17.9	9.4	13.7	37.1
Burke	2242	25.1	78.8	12.0	(29.5)	22.4	87.3
Cavalier	4831	2.9	78.8	13.1	27.4	54.2	107.6
Dickey	5757	21.3	79.6	16.6	28.6	15.4	87.6
Divide	2283	29.5	80.4	13.3	8.1	32.3	57.7
Dunn	3600	17.4	77.5	16.3	48.5	32.1	13.6
Eddy	2757	24.7	75.5	15.9	(14.1)	(10.9)	51.4
Emmons	4331	25.6	65.9	12.3	79.8	45.6	102.2
Golden Valley	1924	21.3	87.4	19.8	4.2	(3.6)	7.9
Grant	2841	24.7	73.4	11.2	31.2	57.8	117.1

Table 2 (Continued)

North Dakota Counties	Population, 2000	Population 65 and older	High-School graduates, 25 and older (%)	Bachelors degree or higher, (%)	Private non-farm employment change, 1990-1999	Per capita income change, 1990-2000 (Negative numbers in parentheses)	Per capita income change, 1980-2000 (Negative numbers in parentheses)
Griggs	2754	25.7	78.7	15.7	69.5	8.1	125.3
Hettinger	2715	25.2	74.8	14.4	(10.6)	65.4	210.8
Kidder	2753	24.0	72.0	11.0	(9.2)	24.5	204.0
La Moure	4701	23.4	75.3	13.9	31.1	18.0	196.9
Logan	2308	27.0	66.0	12.9	(5.8)	25.6	213.4
McHenry	5987	21.8	76.9	13.2	2.0	1.1	46.5
McIntosh	3390	34.2	59.3	9.9	14.8	40.9	134.2
McKenzie	5737	15.7	79.1	15.7	2.2	23.7	13.4
McLean	9311	20.4	79.0	15.1	15.0	7.9	51.7
Mountrail	6631	17.7	77.9	15.6	18.1	18.8	52.4
Nelson	3715	27.4	81.4	17.5	2.2	(13.8)	76.9
Oliver	2065	14.2	79.9	12.0	(8.9)	36.4	57.7
Pierce	4675	24.1	76.7	14.7	19.0	(0.3)	75.2
Renville	2610	22.0	84.1	16.1	34.7	23.2	126.6

Table 2 (Continued)

North Dakota Counties	Population, 2000	Population 65 and older	High-School graduates, 25 and older (%)	Bachelors degree or higher, (%)	Private non-farm employment change, 1990-1999	Per capita income change, 1990-2000 (Negative numbers in parentheses)	Per capita income change, 1980-2000 (Negative numbers in parentheses)
Sargent	4366	16.9	81.1	12.7	26.0	25.5	128.2
Sheridan	1710	26.6	67.8	9.7	83.0	8.6	62.1
Sioux	4044	5.6	78.5	11.2	207.2	22.9	33.7
Slope	767	17.9	82.5	16.0	(18.5)	117.2	334.4
Steele	2258	19.6	86.1	19.8	20.1	(4.9)	230.7
Towner	2876	23.3	81.9	16.1	(5.7)	36.7	107.2
Wells	5102	26.0	72.6	13.7	16.2	(4.2)	60.3
County Average	3768	21.3	77.3	14.5	22.8	22.7	96.6
North Dakota	642200	14.7	83.9	22.0	27.3	18.2	46.1
United States	281.4 million	12.4	80.4	24.4	18.4	21.3	65.4

Sources: U.S. Department of Commerce, Bureau of the Census; U.S. Department of Labor, Bureau of Labor Statistics; USDA, Economic Research Service; U.S. Department of Commerce, Bureau of Economic Analysis.

APPENDIX G. REMOTE OKLAHOMA COUNTIES

Table 1

Oklahoma Counties	Rural-Urban Continuum Code	Urban Influence Code	Population, 2000	Population Change, 1990-2000 (%) (Negative numbers in parentheses)	Population Density (pop/sq.mi.)	Median Household Income ($), 2000	Poverty Rate (%)	Unemployment Rate, 2001 (%)	Average wage per non-farm job, 2000
Beaver	9	9	5857	(2.80)	3.3	$36,715	11.7	2.7	$23,288
Cimarron	9	9	3148	(4.60)	1.8	$30,626	16.6	2.3	$18,257
Dewey	9	9	4743	(14.60)	5.5	$28,172	15	2.7	$19,928
Ellis	9	9	4075	(9.40)	3.7	$27,951	12.5	3.1	$19,845
Grant	9	6	5144	(9.60)	5.7	$28,977	13.7	2.7	$23,796
Harper	8	6	3562	(12.30)	3.9	$33,705	10.2	2.8	$20,529
Roger Mills	9	9	3436	(17.10)	3.6	$30,078	16.3	1.9	$20,855
County Average			4281	(10.06)	3.93	$30,889	13.71	2.6	$20,928
Oklahoma			3.4 million	9.7	50.3	$33,400	14.7	3.8	$26,988
United States			281.4 million	13.1	79.6	$41,994	12.4	4.8	$35,323

Table 2

Oklahoma Counties	Population, 2000	Population 65 and older	High-School graduates, 25 and older (%)	Bachelors degree or higher, (%)	Private non-farm employment change, 1990-1 999	Per capita income change, 1990-2000 (Negative numbers in parentheses)	Per capita income change, 1980-2000 (Negative numbers in parentheses)
Beaver	5857	16.9	81.2	17.6	(0.6)	4.4	(5.7)
Cimarron	3148	18.6	76.6	17.7	34.7	(12.4)	45.9
Dewey	4743	21.0	79.8	16.6	(16.1)	(3.5)	15.0
Ellis	4075	22.0	81.2	19.2	44.7	(3.2)	(1.8)
Grant	5144	21.4	85.7	16.2	(17.9)	(10.0)	11.1
Harper	3562	21.7	82.1	19.2	1.2	11.2	48.1
Roger Mills	3436	18.7	79.3	15.8	43.2	18.4	48.1
County Average	4281	20.0	80.8	17.5	12.7	0.7	23.0
Oklahoma	3.4 million	13.2	80.6	20.3	24.5	10.8	18.1
United States	281.4 million	12.4	80.4	24.4	18.4	21.3	65.4

Sources: U.S. Department of Commerce, Bureau of the Census; U.S. Department of Labor, Bureau of Labor Statistics; USDA, Economic Research Service; U.S. Department of Commerce, Bureau of Economic Analysis.

APPENDIX H. REMOTE SOUTH DAKOTA COUNTIES

Table 1

South Dakota Counties	Rural-Urban Continuum Code	Urban Influence Code	Population, 2000	Population Change, 1990-2000 (%) (Negative numbers in parentheses)	Population Density (pop/sq.mi.)	Median Household Income ($), 2000	Poverty Rate (%)	Unemployment Rate, 2001 (%)	Average wage per non-farm job, 2000
Aurora	9	9	3058	(2.5)	4.4	$29,783	11.4	2.4	$18,915
Bennett	9	9	3074	11.5	2.7	$25,313	39.2	5.9	$20,293
Buffalo	9	9	2032	15.5	3.7	$12,692	56.9	8.4	$24,432
Butte	7	8	9094	14.9	3.5	$29,040	12.8	4.0	$20,001
Campbell	9	9	1782	(9.3)	2.7	$28,793	14.1	6.8	$16,942
Clark	9	9	4143	(5.9)	4.6	$30,208	14.8	7.3	$17,581
Corson	9	9	4181	(0.3)	1.7	$20,654	41.0	8.3	$18,520
Custer	8	6	7275	17.7	4	$36,303	9.4	3.8	$20,588
Dewey	9	9	5972	8.1	2.4	$23,272	33.6	16.1	$22,473
Edmunds	9	9	4367	(0.3)	3.8	$32,205	13.8	2.2	$18,802
Fall River	7	8	7453	1.4	4.2	$29,631	13.6	4.1	$20,871

Table 1 (Continued)

South Dakota Counties	Rural-Urban Continuum Code	Urban Influence Code	Population, 2000	Population Change, 1990-2000 (%) (Negative numbers in parentheses)	Population Density (pop/sq.mi.)	Median Household Income ($), 2000	Poverty Rate (%)	Unemployment Rate, 2001 (%)	Average wage per non-farm job, 2000
Faulk	9	9	2640	(3.8)	2.7	$30,237	18.1	2.7	$17,841
Gregory	9	9	4792	(10.6)	5.3	$22,732	20.1	3.7	$17,887
Haakon	9	9	2196	(16.3)	1.4	$29,894	13.9	2.6	$19,336
Hand	9	9	3741	(12.4)	3	$32,377	9.2	2.2	$17,860
Hanson	9	9	3159	4.8	0.6	$33,049	16.6	2.3	$21,867
Hyde	9	9	1671	(1.5)	2	$31,103	12.3	2.6	$19,347
Jackson	9	9	2930	4.2	1.5	$23,945	36.5	7.0	$18,736
Jerauld	9	9	2295	(5.4)	4.6	$30,690	20.6	2.4	$18,159
Jones	9	9	1193	(9.9)	1.4	$30,288	15.8	1.5	$17,633
Lyman	9	9	3895	7.1	2.2	$28,509	24.3	4.9	$17,230
Marshall	9	9	4576	(5.5)	5.8	$30,567	13.9	7.3	$19,547
McPherson	9	9	2904	(10.0)	2.8	$22,380	22.6	2.3	$15,392
Mellette	9	9	2083	(2.5)	1.6	$23,219	35.8	6.5	$16,274

Table 1 (Continued)

South Dakota Counties	Rural-Urban Continuum Code	Urban Influence Code	Population, 2000	Population Change, 1990-2000 (%) (Negative numbers in parentheses)	Population Density (pop/sq.mi.)	Median Household Income ($), 2000	Poverty Rate (%)	Unemployment Rate, 2001 (%)	Average wage per non-farm job, 2000
Miner	9	9	2884	(11.9)	5.7	$29,519	11.8	5.8	$18,433
Perkins	9	9	3363	(14.5)	1.4	$27,750	16.9	2.7	$17,556
Potter	9	9	2693	(15.6)	3.7	$30,086	12.6	3.6	$17,291
Sanborn	9	9	2675	(5.6)	5	$33,375	14.9	3.4	$15,970
Shannon	7	8	12466	25.9	4.7	$20,916	52.3	12.6	$25,710
Spink	7	8	7454	(6.6)	5.3	$31,717	12.8	3.6	$19,878
Stanley	9	9	2772	13.0	1.7	$41,170	8.7	2.8	$20,458
Sully	9	9	1556	(2.1)	1.6	$32,500	12.1	2.4	$18,265
Todd	9	9	9050	8.5	6	$20,035	48.3	8.3	$21,262
Tripp	7	8	6430	(7.1)	4.3	$28,333	19.9	3.1	$18,847
Ziebach	9	9	2519	13.5	1.1	$18,062	49.9	14.4	$21,593
County Average			4125	(0.4)	3.2	$28,010	22.3	5.1	$19,194
South Dakota			754844	8.5	9.9	$35,282	13.2	3.3	$24,802
United States			281.4 million	13.1	79.6	$41,994	12.4	4.8	$35,323

Table 2

South Dakota Counties	Population, 2000	Population 65 and older	High-School graduates, 25 and older (%)	Bachelors degree or higher, (%)	Private non-farm employment change, 1990-1999	Per capita income change, 1990-2000 (Negative numbers in parentheses)	Per capita income change, 1980-2000 (Negative numbers in parentheses)
Aurora	3058	21.6	79.5	12.7	15.3	16.4	96.6
Bennett	3074	11.1	71.3	12.7	42.3	0.9	33.4
Buffalo	2032	6.5	63.9	5.4	(24.0)	0.4	51.8
Butte	9094	15.2	79.8	12.2	25.0	8.9	5.4
Campbell	1782	22.1	79.2	14.8	32.5	57.8	96.0
Clark	4143	22.2	76.6	11.4	22.0	20.2	73.6
Corson	4181	10.5	76.0	11.3	0.4	36.3	58.2
Custer	7275	16.0	88.9	24.4	0.2	3.1	11.7
Dewey	5972	8.3	77.4	12.2	121.0	25.9	44.0
Edmunds	4367	22.2	73.6	15.5	35.4	26.5	127.3
Fall River	7453	22.5	82.5	19.2	54.1	19.6	8.7
Faulk	2640	22.9	73.7	13.1	40.3	27.0	103.5
Gregory	4792	24.8	77.7	12.0	13.5	14.8	51.0

Table 2 (Continued)

South Dakota Counties	Population, 2000	Population 65 and older	High-School graduates, 25 and older (%)	Bachelors degree or higher, (%)	Private non-farm employment change, 1990-1999	Per capita income change, 1990-2000 (Negative numbers in parentheses)	Per capita income change, 1980-2000 (Negative numbers in parentheses)
Haakon	2196	18.0	86.3	15.4	20.5	22.7	87.7
Hand	3741	24.2	80.1	15.6	7.0	12.2	58.5
Hanson	3159	14.9	75.1	14.0	20.1	34.6	107.0
Hyde	1671	22.3	80.5	16.0	61.2	7.7	69.0
Jackson	2930	11.6	82.7	16.2	30.4	(0.7)	58.9
Jerauld	2295	25.6	79.6	12.3	15.7	11.2	108.9
Jones	1193	18.2	86.2	17.8	32.9	(0.7)	35.5
Lyman	3895	13.6	81.1	15.9	46.1	4.1	91.9
Marshall	4576	21.3	75.6	16.2	49.0	13.0	96.9
McPherson	2904	29.6	58.8	10.7	(8.5)	14.2	65.8
Mellette	2083	13.2	78.1	16.6	126.5	(5.6)	19.5
Miner	2884	23.9	79.6	13.5	(9.0)	16.0	92.2
Perkins	3363	23.7	80.3	14.6	(7.6)	5.7	46.4
Potter	2693	25.0	80.8	16.2	65.2	59.9	127.3

Table 2 (Continued)

South Dakota Counties	Population, 2000	Population 65 and older	High-School graduates, 25 and older (%)	Bachelors degree or higher, (%)	Private non-farm employment change, 1990-1999	Per capita income change, 1990-2000 (Negative numbers in parentheses)	Per capita income change, 1980-2000 (Negative numbers in parentheses)
Sanborn	2675	19.5	82.7	14.8	26.8	30.4	110.3
Shannon	12466	4.8	70.0	12.1	53.8	34.3	51.8
Spink	7454	18.9	81.4	14.4	9.0	14.0	96.8
Stanley	2772	11.0	87.7	22.1	70.9	35.9	47.1
Sully	1556	17.4	84.9	16.4	8.1	13.5	197.5
Todd	9050	5.8	74.1	12.1	50.1	32.8	30.0
Tripp	6430	19.7	80.2	13.5	25.7	4.2	43.5
Ziebach	2519	7.5	71.4	12.0	49.0	(19.6)	(15.8)
County Average	4125	17.6	78.2	14.4	32.0	17.1	68.2
South Dakota	754844	14.3	84.6	21.5	37.2	21.4	52.6
United States	281.4 million	12.4	80.4	24.4	18.4	21.3	65.4

Sources: U.S. Department of Commerce, Bureau of the Census; U.S. Department of Labor, Bureau of Labor Statistics; USDA, Economic Research Service; U.S. Department of Commerce, Bureau of Economic Analysis.

APPENDIX I. REMOTE TEXAS COUNTIES

Table 1

Texas Counties	Rural-Urban Continuum Code	Urban Influence Code	Population, 2000	Population Change, 1990-2000 (%) (Negative numbers in parentheses)	Population Density (pop/sq.mi.)	Median Household Income ($), 2000	Poverty Rate (%)	Unemployment Rate, 2001 (%)	Average wage per non-farm job, 2000
Armstrong	8	6	2,148	6.3	2.2	$39,194	10.6	1.3	$25,776
Baylor	7	8	4,093	(6.7)	5.0	$24,627	16.1	4.2	$19,654
Borden	9	9	729	(8.8)	0.9	$29,205	14.0	2.0	$25,395
Brewster	7	8	8,866	2.5	1.4	$27,386	18.2	2.2	$21,549
Briscoe	9	9	1,790	(9.2)	2.2	$29,917	16.0	2.7	$18,747
Cochran	7	8	3,730	(14.8)	5.6	$27,525	27.0	6.5	$21,645
Coke	8	6	3,864	12.9	3.8	$29,085	13.0	1.9	$21,997
Collingsworth	9	9	3,206	(10.3)	3.9	$25,437	18.7	1.1	$21,802
Concho	8	6	3,966	(15.3)	3.1	$25,446	18.4	5.0	$26,876
Cottle	9	9	1,904	30.3	2.5	$31,312	11.9	1.9	$19,761
Crane	6	6	3,996	(14.1)	5.9	$32,194	13.4	6.0	$31,329
Crockett	7	7	4,099	0.5	1.5	$29,355	19.4	2.6	$21,252

Table 1 (Continued)

Texas Counties	Rural-Urban Continuum Code	Urban Influence Code	Population, 2000	Population Change, 1990-2000 (%) (Negative numbers in parentheses)	Population Density (pop/sq.mi.)	Median Household Income ($), 2000	Poverty Rate (%)	Unemployment Rate, 2001 (%)	Average wage per non-farm job, 2000
Culberson	7	8	2,975	(12.7)	0.9	$25,882	25.1	7.6	$18,935
Dallam	7	8	6,222	13.9	3.6	$27,946	14.1	2.2	$24,966
Dickens	9	9	2,962	7.4	2.8	$25,898	17.4	3.1	$22,250
Donley	9	9	3,828	3.6	4.0	$29,006	15.9	2.6	$18,789
Edwards	9	9	2,162	(4.6)	1.1	$25,298	31.6	4.6	$21,062
Fisher	9	8	4,344	(10.3)	5.4	$27,659	17.5	3.2	$21,151
Foard	9	9	1,622	(9.6)	2.5	$25,812	14.3	2.8	$16,897
Garza	6	6	4,872	(5.3)	5.7	$27,206	22.3	2.5	$22,592
Glasscock	8	6	1,406	(2.8)	1.6	$35,655	14.7	3.0	$22,661
Hall	9	9	3,782	(3.1)	4.3	$23,016	26.3	4.2	$17,922
Hartley	7	8	5,537	52.4	2.5	$46,327	6.6	1.2	$22,852
Hemphill	9	9	3,351	(9.9)	4.1	$35,456	12.6	1.7	$26,630
Hudspeth	8	6	3,344	14.7	0.6	$21,045	35.8	4.3	$24,227
Irion	8	6	1,771	8.7	1.5	$37,500	8.4	2.3	$28,254

Table 1

Texas Counties	Rural-Urban Continuum Code	Urban Influence Code	Population, 2000	Population Change, 1990–2000 (%) (Negative numbers in parentheses)	Population Density (pop/sq.mi.)	Median Household Income ($), 2000	Poverty Rate (%)	Unemployment Rate, 2001 (%)	Average wage per non-farm job, 2000
Jeff Davis	9	9	2,207	13.4	0.9	$32,212	15.0	1.8	$21,340
Jim Hogg	6	6	5,281	3.4	4.5	$25,833	25.9	4.5	$20,361
Kenedy	9	9	414	(10.0)	0.3	$25,000	15.3	1.8	$19,983
Kent	9	9	859	(15.0)	1.1	$30,433	10.4	2.0	$20,354
Kimble	7	8	4,468	8.4	3.3	$29,396	18.8	1.7	$18,812
King	7	8	356	0.6	0.4	$35,625	20.7	3.8	$31,445
Kenney	9	9	3,379	8.3	2.3	$28,320	24.0	6.3	$22,267
Knox	9	9	4,253	(12.1)	5.7	$20,665	22.9	3.3	$21,693
La Salle	6	6	5,866	11.6	3.5	$21,857	29.8	6.2	$23,579
Lipscomb	9	9	3,057	(2.7)	3.4	$31,964	16.7	2.0	$25,457
Loving	9	9	67	(37.4)	0.2	$40,000	0.0	7.9	$36,569
Martin	6	5	4,746	(4.2)	5.4	$31,836	18.7	4.1	$25,665
Mason	9	9	3,738	9.2	3.7	$30,921	13.2	1.6	$19,578
McMullen	9	9	851	4.2	0.7	$32,500	20.7	3.1	$31,205

Table 1

Texas Counties	Rural-Urban Continuum Code	Urban Influence Code	Population, 2000	Population Change, 1990-2000 (%) (Negative numbers in parentheses)	Population Density (pop/sq.mi.)	Median Household Income ($), 2000	Poverty Rate (%)	Unemployment Rate, 2001 (%)	Average wage per non-farm job, 2000
Menard	8	6	2,360	4.8	2.5	$24,762	25.8	4.0	$18,031
Motley	9	9	1,426	(6.9)	1.5	$28,348	19.4	1.7	$18,846
Oldham	8	6	2,185	(4.1)	1.5	$33,713	19.8	1.4	$22,073
Pecos	7	8	16,809	14.5	3.1	$28,033	20.4	5.0	$22,994
Presidio	7	8	7,304	10.0	1.7	$19,860	36.4	23.5	$21,236
Reagan	6	6	3,326	(26.3)	3.8	$33,231	11.8	3.0	$24,434
Real	9	9	3,047	26.3	3.4	$25,118	21.2	3.8	$15,165
Reeves	7	7	13,137	(17.1)	6.0	$23,306	28.9	6.8	$18,204
Roberts	9	9	887	(13.5)	1.1	$44,792	7.2	1.5	$20,430
San Saba	7	8	6,186	14.5	4.8	$30,104	16.6	2.9	$20,451
Schleicher	8	6	2,935	(1.8)	2.3	$29,746	21.5	2.3	$21,094
Shackleford	8	6	3,302	(0.4)	3.6	$30,479	13.6	2.2	$23,488
Sherman	9	9	3,186	11.5	3.1	$33,179	16.8	1.5	$22,448
Sterling	8	6	1,393	(3.1)	1.6	$35,129	19.3	3.8	$21,282

Table 1

Texas Counties	Rural-Urban Continuum Code	Urban Influence Code	Population, 2000	Population Change, 1990-2000 (%) (Negative numbers in parentheses)	Population Density (pop/sq.mi.)	Median Household Income ($), 2000	Poverty Rate (%)	Unemployment Rate, 2001 (%)	Average wage per non-farm job, 2000
Stonewall	9	9	1,693	(15.9)	2.2	$27,935	18.0	4.7	$21,153
Sutton	7	8	4,077	(1.4)	2.8	$34,385	25.2	2.8	$24,289
Terrell	9	9	1,081	(23.3)	0.6	$24,219	13.5	3.0	$23,783
Throckmorton	9	9	1,850	(1.6)	2.1	$28,277	19.9	2.1	$18,746
Upton	8	6	3,404	(23.5)	3.6	$28,977		4.1	$28,407
County Average			3,554	(1.1)	2.8	$29,569	18.4	3.6	$22,540
Texas			20.8 million	22.8	79.6	$39,927	15.4	4.9	$34,941
United States			281.4 million	13.1	79.6	$41,994	12.4	4.8	$35,323

Table 2

Texas Counties	Population, 2000	Population 65 and older	High-School graduates, 25 and older (%)	Bachelors degree or higher, (%)	Private non-farm employment change, 1990-1	Per capita income change, 1990-2000 (Negative numbers in parentheses)	Per capita income change, 1980-2000 (Negative numbers in parentheses)
Armstrong	2148	19.2	82.4	20.5	NA	(5.8)	(19.2)
Baylor	4093	24.1	70.1	12.1	40.7	(3.6)	(5.5)
Borden	729	16.3	83.9	21.4	NA	(39.4)	(52.3)
Brewster	8866	14.6	78.6	27.7	28.8	28.3	21.5
Briscoe	1790	19.3	74.8	17.5	(7.9)	(6.0)	43.4
Cochran	3730	14.4	62.7	10.2	9.6	3.8	123.3
Coke	3864	24.1	74.2	14.7	67.8	2.6	5.3
Collingsworth	3206	22.0	71.3	15.3	(3.8)	2.1	73.0
Concho	3966	13.8	59.3	14.1	89.9	15.9	3.6
Cottle	1904	25.6	66.1	15.3	49.2	(23.1)	44.5
Crane	3996	10.9	68.7	12.8	(27.5)	7.5	(12.8)
Crockett	4099	12.9	62.1	10.4	26.8	(10.4)	(1.3)
Culberson	2975	11.2	56.1	13.9	31.6	21.3	(8.2)
Dallam	6222	10.3	65.0	9.6	38.9	24.1	88.5

Table 2

Texas Counties	Population, 2000	Population 65 and older	High-School graduates, 25 and older (%)	Bachelors degree or higher, (%)	Private non-farm employment change, 1990-1	Per capita income change, 1990-2000 (Negative numbers in parentheses)	Per capita income change, 1980-2000 (Negative numbers in parentheses)
Dickens	2962	19.0	70.6	8.4	26.0	(5.8)	17.8
Donley	3828	21.7	78.2	15.8	(17.6)	(8.4)	16.8
Edwards	2162	16.2	67.1	17.3	(31.7)	3.1	(0.1)
Fisher	4344	22.7	73.3	12.4	15.7	(4.0)	14.3
Foard	1622	23.1	70.0	10.5	(6.2)	(3.4)	28.5
Garza	4872	14.1	70.1	10.0	(2.6)	22.8	25.8
Glasscock	1406	9.0	69.9	18.7	117.2	(20.3)	74.5
Hall	3782	21.5	61.7	9.1	81.9	(11.5)	(31.8)
Hartley	5537	11.9	77.3	17.6	158.8	(8.2)	48.4
Hemphill	3351	14.7	79.9	17.9	14.7	39.3	96.1
Hudspeth	3344	9.9	46.1	9.7	25.0	26.1	22.0
Irion	1771	15.6	78.8	21.5	(16.4)	(5.8)	(12.2)
Jeff Davis	2207	16.3	74.7	35.1	53.4	(3.4)	(19.4)
Jim Hogg	5281	14.6	58.0	9.5	28.0	10.1	1.7

Table 2

Texas Counties	Population, 2000	Population 65 and older	High-School graduates, 25 and older (%)	Bachelors degree or higher, (%)	Private non-farm employment change, 1990-1	Per capita income change, 1990-2000 (Negative numbers in parentheses)	Per capita income change, 1980-2000 (Negative numbers in parentheses)
Kenedy	414	10.6	57.9	20.3	NA	9.3	22.0
Kent	859	25.5	78.1	15.1	162.2	42.2	68.0
Kimble	4468	20.9	72.1	17.3	23.0	(2.0)	(4.6)
King	356	10.4	78.1	24.6	NA	21.1	36.0
Kinney	3379	24.3	66.9	17.7	(26.1)	30.1	37.5
Knox	4253	22.7	66.8	11.8	(7.7)	10.4	40.8
La Salle	5866	11.6	50.1	6.4	49.6	23.7	84.0
Lipscomb	3057	18.4	74.5	18.9	17.4	(4.3)	30.3
Loving	67	16.4	86.3	5.9	NA	105.7	53.8
Martin	4746	13.3	65.8	11.8	16.7	(12.9)	47.7
Mason	3738	23.5	78.1	18.7	(19.3)	(6.0)	15.5
McMullen	851	17.9	74.7	16.2	(13.7)	24.7	43.7
Menard	2360	21.9	69.4	17.2	47.6	0.3	(2.3)
Motley	1426	23.7	73.5	14.7	(7.1)	(23.6)	(3.3)

Table 2

Texas Counties	Population, 2000	Population 65 and older	High-School graduates, 25 and older (%)	Bachelors degree or higher, (%)	Private non-farm employment change, 1990-1	Per capita income change, 1990-2000 (Negative numbers in parentheses)	Per capita income change, 1980-2000 (Negative numbers in parentheses)
Oldham	2185	11.3	80.5	19.4	206.4	4.2	117.5
Pecos	16809	10.8	62.5	12.9	9.5	2.5	(6.0)
Presidio	7304	13.9	44.7	11.7	7.0	16.8	(3.4)
Reagan	3326	10.3	63.0	9.2	14.7	10.4	0.8
Real	3047	20.8	73.0	17.3	128.2	13.0	53.2
Reeves	13137	12.6	46.8	8.0	3.8	19.9	4.4
Roberts	887	14.4	90.0	25.4	(46.3)	(10.7)	1.0
San Saba	6186	20.3	70.0	15.8	(12.9)	2.6	15.7
Schleicher	2935	16.4	60.4	17.6	50.4	5.8	(9.2)
Shackelford	3302	18.2	79.2	20.8	(23.5)	(3.1)	28.0
Sherman	3186	13.6	73.1	20.4	7.1	(2.3)	64.8
Sterling	1393	14.6	70.4	17.1	(16.7)	19.2	(8.5)
Stonewall	1693	24.0	71.0	12.6	12.6	(1.8)	20.2
Sutton	4077	12.5	64.4	13.0	37.5	5.9	13.8

Table 2

Texas Counties	Population, 2000	Population 65 and older	High-School graduates, 25 and older (%)	Bachelors degree or higher, (%)	Private non-farm employment change, 1990-1	Per capita income change, 1990-2000 (Negative numbers in parentheses)	Per capita income change, 1980-2000 (Negative numbers in parentheses)
Terrell	1081	17.7	70.9	19.0	(33.7)	26.9	61.3
Throckmorton	1850	20.5	77.4	18.2	42.0	(27.7)	22.4
Upton	3404	14.2	67.1	11.8	(4.3)	5.2	2.4
County Average	3554	16.9	69.6	15.5	26.2	6.0	24.3
Texas	20.8 million	9.9	75.7	23.2	32.4	20.7	33.4
United States	281.4 million	12.4	80.4	24.4	18.4	21.3	65.4

Sources: U.S. Department of Commerce, Bureau of the Census; U.S. Department of Labor, Bureau of Labor Statistics; USDA, Economic Research Service; U.S. Department of Commerce, Bureau of Economic Analysis.

REFERENCES

[1]   U.S. economic activity is overwhelmingly concentrated along the country's ocean coasts and Great Lakes coasts, as well as its navigable rivers. See Jordan Rappaport and Jeffrey Sachs, "The United States as a Coastal Nation," Center for International Development, Harvard University, July 2001.

[2]   See Walter Prescott Webb, *The Great Plains* (Blaisdell Publishing Co.: Waltham, Mass., 1931); James R. Dickenson, *Home on the Range: A Century on the High Plains* (New York: Scribner, 1995).

[3]   This result has led to the counter-argument to Turner that the U.S. frontier not only remains but is growing. See Deborah E. Popper and Frank Popper, "The Great Plains: From Dust to Dust," *Planning* 53, no. 12, 1987.

[4]   For statistical details concerning the Census Bureau's formal definitions of rural and urban, see *Federal Register*, vol. 67, no. 51, March 15, 2002, pp. 11663-11670. In June 2003, the Office of Management and Budget promulgated revised definitions of Metropolitan Statistical Areas (MSAs). See *OMB Bulletin* no.03-04, June 6, 2003.

[5]   John Cromartie, "Measuring Rurality: What Is Rural?" USDA-ERS Briefing Room, 2003, [http://www.ers.usda.gov/Briefing/Rurality].

[6]   The Bureau of the Census and Office of Management and Budget definitions are created solely for the purposes of demographic measurement and analysis. Keenly aware that this purpose can conflict with policies that target specific populations and geographic regions, these agencies have long recommended and encouraged other agencies that use their definitions to modify them to serve the objectives of their particular programs. See *Federal Register*, vol.65, no. 249, December 27, 2000, pp. 82228-82238.

[7]   Most (91%) metro county residents are urban area residents.

[8]   Appendix A describes two widely used scales developed by USDA's Economic Research Service (ERS) that measure rural non-metropolitan counties by their population, their proximity to metropolitan areas, and the relative size of population centers within the non-metro county. In addition, Appendix A also describes two ERS typologies that categorize non-metro counties on the basis of economic and policy types.

[9]   Farming-dependent counties are defined by USDA as those where 20% or more of total labor and proprietors' income stems from

agriculture. Inflation adjusted total personal income in farm-dependent counties grew 13% between 1990 and 1998, compared to 21% growth in other non-metro counties. See Fred Gale, "How Important Are Farm Payments to the Rural Economy?" *Agriculture Outlook*, October 2000.

[10] The other eight most highly ranked rural problems, in descending order, are access to healthcare, low-wage jobs, quality of education, sprawl, access to technology, access to transportation, breakup of the family, and the environment. See W. K. Kellogg Foundation, *Perception of Rural America: National State Legislator Survey*, Battle Creek, MI, November 2002.

[11] Richard Reeder, F. Bagi, and S. Calhous, "Who's Vulnerable to Federal Budget Cuts?" *Rural Development Perspectives* 11(2), June 1996.

[12] See Karl N. Stauber, *"Why Invest in Rural America — and How? A Critical Public Policy Question for the 21st Century."* Paper presented at Exploring Policy Options for a New Rural America, Center for the Study of Rural America, Kansas City Federal Reserve Bank, May 2001.

[13] ome observers even argue that the United States has now entered a "post-suburban" era of development. See Rob Kling, Spencer Olin, and Mark Poster, *Postsuburban California: The Transformation of Orange County Since World War II*, (Berkeley: University of California Press, 1995).

[14] Ibid.

[15] See General Accounting Office, *Rural Development: Patchwork of Federal Programs Needs to Be Reappraised*, GAO/RCED-94-165, July 1994.

[16] USDA Economic Research Service calculation from Census of Population data, U.S. Bureau of the Census.

[17] John Cromartie, "Non-metro Migration Drops in the West and Among College Graduates," USDA-ERS, *Rural Conditions and Trends*, 11(2), December 2000.

[18] Jack Runyan, "Farm Labor: Demographic Characteristics of Hired Farmworkers," USDA-ERS Briefing Room, 2003, [http://www.ers.usda.gov/Briefing/FarmLabor/Demographics/].

[19] For an overview of rural population trends, see [http://www.ers.usda.gov/Briefing/ Population].

[20] A recent analysis of rural population growth rates showed that rates varied greatly across counties and across decades. Interestingly, the research showed that only about 20% of the variance in population

growth could not be attributed to state- or national-level variables, leaving nearly 80% of the variance that must be explained by variables that vary across or within counties. See Tzu-Ling Huang, P. Orazem, and D. Wohlgemuth, "Rural Population Growth, 1950-1990: The Roles of Human Capital Industry, Structure, and Government Policy," *American Journal of Agricultural Economics* 84, no. 3 (2002), pp. 615-627.

[21] Ibid., p.29.

[22] See John Cromartie, "Non-Metro Migration Drops in the West and Among College Graduates," USDA-ERS, *Rural Conditions and Trends*, 11(2), December 2000; Daniel Lichter et al., "Migration and the Loss of Human Resources in Rural Areas," in *Investing in People: The Human Capital Needs of Rural America*, ed. L. J. Beaulieu and D. Mulkey (Boulder: Westview Press, 1995).

[23] Based on U.S. Bureau of the Census measures of poverty, farm-dependent counties (see definition, page 35), while still having relatively high rates of poverty (an average of 15.7% in 1999), saw the largest decline in county poverty rates of the various ERS county economic classifications from 1989-1999, probably due to relatively larger farm payments and relatively strong national economy. The Census measures the poverty rate by establishing poverty thresholds, i.e., the dollar amounts used to determine poverty status. Each person or family is assigned one out of 48 possible poverty thresholds. Thresholds vary according to size of the family and ages of the household members. The same thresholds are used throughout the United States and updated annually for inflation using the Consumer Price Index for all urban consumers.

[24] Dean Joliffe, "Non-Metro Poverty: Assessing the Effects of the 1990s," *Amber Waves*, USDA-ERS, June 2003.

[25] Ibid.

[26] See CRS Report 95-1081, *Education Matters: Earnings by Highest Year of Schooling Completed.*

[27] See CRS Report 97-764, *The Skill (Education) Distribution of Jobs: How Is It Changing?*

[28] Lief Jenson and D. McLaughlin, "Human Capital and Non-metropolitan Poverty," in L. J. Beaulieu and D. Mulkey (eds.), *Investing in People: The Human Capital Needs of Rural America* (Boulder, CO: Westview Press, 1995).

[29] Earnings, income, rates of poverty, education and training, etc., are factors both of the characteristics of the labor force and of an area's

industrial structure. They can be analyzed separately, but the economic characteristics of an area result from both the organization of labor supply and the economic structure of labor demand within a region.

[30] Some research suggests that this poses a paradox in regard to public policies aimed at raising the level of human capital in rural areas. A times series analysis of rural areas showed that rural population growth was affected most by improvements in human capital stock over time. Because urban returns to education appear to be higher than those of rural areas, increasing the rural human capital stock actually decreased the working-age population, largely because more educated labor moved elsewhere. See Tzu-Ling Huang, P. Orazem, and D. Wohlgemuth, "Rural Population Growth, 1950-1990: The Roles of Human Capital Industry, Structure, and Government Policy," *American Journal of Agricultural Economics* 84, no. 3 (2002), pp. 615-627.

[31] Robert Gibbs, "Rural Labor and Education: Rural Education," USDA-ERS Briefing Room, 2003. See [http://www.ers.usda.gov/Briefing/LaborandEducation].

[32] Data were based on Bureau of Economic Analysis personal income data adjusted for inflation with the implicit price deflator for personal consumption expenses. See Rural Sociological Society Task Force on Persistent Rural Poverty, *Persistent Rural Poverty in Rural America* (Boulder, CO: Westview Press, 1993).

[33] See Jill L. Findies and L. Jensen, "Employment Opportunities in Rural Areas: Implications for Poverty in a Changing Environment," *American Journal of Agricultural Economics* 80 (1998), pp. 1000-1007.

[34] Ibid.

[35] Douglas Rhoades and Mitch Renkow, "Explaining Rural-Urban Earnings Differentials in the United States," paper presented at the Annual Meeting of the American Agricultural Economics Association, Salt Lake City, Utah, 1998, *American Journal of Agricultural Economics* 80 (5), p. 1172. A study of rural and urban North Carolina counties also showed that rural areas had both lower rates of return to schooling and a greater sensitivity of earnings to local labor market conditions than urban counties, although national macroeconomic trends had the dominant impact on both metro and non-metro counties. See Mark Renkow, "Rural versus Urban Growth: Why Do Rural Counties Lag Behind?" Center for Regional Development, North

Carolina State University, 1995 ([http://www.ces.ncsu.edu/resources/economics/crdnews/]).

[36] See Jill L. Findies and L. Jensen, "Employment Opportunities in Rural Areas: Implications for Poverty in a Changing Environment," *American Journal of Agricultural Economics* 80 (1998), pp. 1000-1007; Jill L. Findeis, "Gender Differences in Human Capital in Rural America," in Lionel Beaulieu and David Mulkey (eds.), *Investing in People: The Human Capital Needs of Rural America* (Boulder, CO: Westview Press, 1995); Tim Parker and Leslie Whitener, "Minimum Wage Legislation: Rural Workers Will Benefit More than Urban Workers from Increase in Minimum Wage," USDA-ERS, *Rural Conditions and Trends* 8 (1), 1997.

[37] Constance Newman, *Impacts of Hispanic Population Growth on Rural Wages*, USDA. AER-826, September 2003.

[38] Linda M. Ghelfi, "Rural Per Capita Income Grows Slightly More than Urban," USDA-ERS, *Rural Conditions and Trends* 9 (2), 1997.

[39] In the study's sample, at least 41% of all workers in these 465 counties were employed in industries paying average wages that would not lift a full-time, full-year worker above the weighted-average poverty threshold for a family of four ($15,569 in 1995). Average wages were calculated for each three-digit Standard Industrial Code (SIC) industry in each county rather than assuming a single average for each industry. See Robert Gibbs and J. B. Cromartie, "Low-wage Counties Face Locational Disadvantages," USDA-ERS, *Rural Conditions and Trends* 11 (2), 2000.

[40] The low-wage counties that are dependent on manufacturing tend to be located in the rural South. Similarly, all mining-dependent low-wage counties are in the West.

[41] Some observers point to cost-of-living differences between rural and urban areas to account for earnings differentials or to account for price differences when comparing standards of living between geographic areas. Conceptual and measurement issues in developing indexes that might estimate geographic cost-of-living are significant. Commonly accepted measures such as Bureau of Labor Statistics Family Budget Studies, the American Chamber of Commerce Researchers Association Cost of Living Index, and the Bureau of Labor Statistics city Consumer Price Indexes generally focus on metropolitan areas. Rural areas, in particular, are excluded from these calculated measures. See Laura A. Blanciforti and Edit Kranner, "Estimating County Cost of Living Indexes: The Issue of Urban versus Rural,"

Research Paper 9718, West Virginia Regional Research Institute, 1997. For an analysis of the conceptual and measurement complexities of cost-of-living indexes, see National Academy of Sciences, *At What Price: Conceptualizing and Measuring Cost-of-Living and Price Indexes* (Washington, D.C.: National Academy Press, 2002). One study of rural and urban residents in Wisconsin concluded that metro and non-metro households spent about the same on such essentials as food, clothing, transportation, utilities, and medical care (although in the National Academy of Sciences study cited above, constructing an index for medical care proved more difficult than any other component of the Consumer Price Index). Non-metro residents lived on less income largely because they were disproportionately elderly and had higher concentrations of households with paid-up mortgages than metro areas. See Linda M. Ghelfi, "About That Lower Cost of Living in Non-Metro Areas," USDA-ERS, *Rural Development Perspectives*, October 1988.

[42] "Persistently poor" counties are defined by ERS as those counties with 20% or more of their population with poverty level incomes in each of four years 1960, 1970, 1980, and 1990.

[43] U.S. Census of Agriculture, *Ranking of States and Counties*, vol. 2, part 2, 1997.

[44] See Rick Reeder, F. Bagi, and S. Calhoun, "Which Federal Programs Are Most Important for the Great Plains?" USDA-ERS, *Rural Development Perspectives*, vol. 13. no. 1, June 1998.

[45] See footnote 9, above. The ERS county classification defines "government-dependent" counties as those where at least 25% of total county income comes from government. See Appendix A for ERS county profiles.

[46] Community resource funding supports economic development, community facilities, environmental protection, housing, and transportation. Compared with non-metro counties nationally, non-metro Great Plains counties receive 32% more in community resources..

[47] Only approximately 13% of farm households receive more than 80% of their household income from farming. See Ashock Mishra and M. Morehart, "Farm Families' Savings: Findings from the Arms Survey," *Agricultural Outlook*, April 2002.

[48] Edwin S. Mills, "The Location of Economic Activity in Rural and Non-Metropolitan United States," in E.N. Castle (ed.), *The Changing*

American Countryside, (Lawrence: University of Kansas Press, 1995), pp. 103-133.

[49] Michael D. Boehlje, Steven L. Hofing, and R. Christopher Schroeder, *Farming in the 21ˢᵗ Century*, Staff Paper # 99-9, Department of Economics, Purdue University, 1999.

[50] National Corn Growers Association, *Changes in the Evolution of Corn Belt Agriculture*, February 2002.

[51] Mark Drabenstott, "Rural America in a New Century," *Main Street Economist*, Federal Reserve Bank of Kansas City, October 1999.

[52] USDA-ERS, *Agricultural Resource Management Study*, 1998.

[53] Ibid.

[54] Mark Drabenstott and L. G. Meeker, "Consolidation in U.S. Agriculture: The New Rural Landscape and Public Policy," *Economic Review*, Kansas City Federal Reserve, October 1999.

[55] G. Benjamin, "Industrialization in Hog Production: Implications for Midwest Agriculture," *Economic Perspectives*, Federal Reserve Bank of Chicago, 1997.

[56] Opposition to these industrialization trends is also widespread because concentration and consolidation in the agro-food industry continues to be regarded as a significant threat to the survival of small family farms. See, for example, William Heffernan, *Consolidation in the Food and Agriculture System*, Report to the National Farmers Union, February 1999.

[57] See *Agriculture as a Tool for Rural Development: Workshop Proceedings*, Henry A. Wallance Center for Agricultural and Environmental Policy, April 2003.

[58] Nontraditional crops, new agricultural production techniques, small-scale processing facilities, and bio-fuel plants may offer rural areas new ways of integrating agriculture into local economies. See CRS Report RL31598, *Value-Added Agricultural Enterprises in Rural Development Strategies*.

[59] Some programs do exist. A portion of Farm Security Agency loans are earmarked each year for beginning farmers.

[60] The "treadmill effect" refers to technology and its influence on agricultural production. In the quest for a safe, plentiful, and inexpensive food supply, land grant universities and a public support system promote this as a public good. Advancements in technology create the "treadmill effect" for agricultural producers by continuously requiring the systematic adoption of new technology in order to remain competitive. In turn, this systematic adoption of technology

either reduces or holds prices down for farmers while it increases their cost of production. Producers who fail to adopt new technology lose their competitive advantage. Producers who adopt new technology are often rewarded with even lower prices and a narrower profit margin. See Willard Cochrane, *The Development of American Agriculture: A Historical Analysis*, 2nd ed., (Minneapolis: University of Minnesota Press, 1993).

[61] *Overview of Transportation Infrastructure and Services in the Northern Great Plains*, report prepared for the Northern Great Plains Regional Authority by the Northeast-Midwest Institute, 2000.

[62] The Commission on the Future of the United States Aerospace Industry was established by Section 1092 of the Floyd D. Spence National Defense Authorization Act of 2002. The Commission was formed to study the future of the United States aerospace industry in the global economy, particularly in relationship to United States national security; and to assess the future importance of the domestic aerospace industry for the economic and national security of the United States.

[63] For a selective overview of five case studies of regional development organizations, see *Multi-Region Economic Development Strategies Guide: Case Studies in Multi-Region Cooperation to Promote Economic Development*, National Association of Regional Councils, 2000.

[64] Andrew Isserman and T. Rephann, "The Economic Effects of the Appalachian Regional Commission: An Empirical Assessment of 26 Years of Regional Development Planning," *Journal of the American Planning Association* 61 (3), summer 1995.

[65] Chuck Hassebrook, testimony on rural development before the Senate Agriculture, Nutrition, and Forestry Committee, 107th Congress, 2nd session, August 2, 2001.

[66] This is not to imply that economic criteria are the only or even the most important basis for making economic development decisions. While market forces remain the dominant means of allocating resources and wealth in the United States, they have never been the sole means of making policy decisions.

[67] Michael Lind, "The new Continental Divide," *The Atlantic Monthly*, January-February 2003.

[68] In contrast, Europe has embraced relatively ambitious regional programs. This regional emphasis in Europe may reflect more pronounced disparities between urban areas and rural regions there

compared to the United States. Most recently, one can see this policy difference in the EU's Common Agricultural Policy reforms, where rural development is one of the three central pillars of agricultural reform.

[69] Some regional development analysts have argued that making areas attractive to the "creative classes" is a necessary ingredient for successful economic development in the future. Conventional economic development models may no longer suffice. Focusing more on why certain cities are declining and others thriving, these observers cite the importance of making adaptations in local cultures to attract and retain creative class employees. Business have begun doing this, but civic leaders have generally not grasped that what is true for corporations may also be true for cities and regions. See Richard Florida, *The Rise of the Creative Class* (New York: Basic Books, 2002). In contrast, other analysts have argued that the statistical evidence for the role of the "creative class" is far less convincing. See Steve Malanga, "The Curse of the Creative Class," *City Journal*, vol. 14 (1), winter 2004.

[70] It is also the case that what rural researchers often think is effective might be otherwise. In a late 1980s study of 548 non-metro counties, researchers for the National Governors' Association were surprised to learn that 13 variables widely thought to be important factors in differentiating communities that grew from those that did not (e.g., change in employment, federal spending on development, county population, adjacency to a metro area) could only explain about 17% of the growth that actually occurred. See Sandra S. Batie, DeWitt John, and Kim Norris, *A Brighter Future for Rural America? Strategies for Communities and States* (Washington, D.C.: National Governors' Association, 1988).

[71] See David Freshwater, "What Can Social Scientists Contribute to the Challenges of Rural Economic Development?" *Journal of Agricultural and Applied Economics* 32 (2), August 2000.

[72] Ibid., p.348.

[73] The data here are quite old. This table provides a general distributional picture that may still be valid, although the counties falling into each category have likely changed. For example, in 1999, ERS reported that there were 312 farming-dependent counties, a decline of 44% since 1989.

[74] Some researchers regard the city as the essential engine of development. See Jane Jacobs, *The Economy of Cities* (1969) and *Cities and the Wealth of Nations* (1984).

In: Rural Development   ISBN 978-1-60021-161-4
Editors:T.Cowan, B.Foote, pp.141-147© 2007 Nova Science Publishers, Inc.

Chapter 3

RURAL HOUSING: USDA DISASTER RELIEF PROVISIONS[*]

Bruce E. Foote

SUMMARY

When disasters occur, such as Hurricane Katrina, the U.S. Department of Agriculture (USDA) provides housing relief to residents of the affected areas in general and to affected participants in the various USDA rural housing programs. This report provides an overview of those housing relief efforts. Assistance can be placed in three broad categories: (1) relief for homeowners and homebuyers; (2) relief for apartment dwellers; and (3) and relief for multi-family property owners.

For Section 521 rental assistance allocated to housing made uninhabitable by Hurricane Katrina or Hurricane Rita, H.R. 3895, as passed by the House on October 6, 2005, would amend the Housing Act of 1949 to permit the conversion of the rental assistance into either Section 8 vouchers or rural housing vouchers. The bill would amend the law to permit Section 502 guarantee loans to be used for the repair or rehabilitation of existing properties.

---

[*] Excerpted from CRS Report RS22301, dated October 18, 2005.

Title V of the Housing Act of 1949 (42 U.S.C. 1471 et seq.), as amended, authorizes the U.S. Department of Agriculture (USDA) to administer several programs which provide housing opportunities to residents of rural areas. The programs are administered by the Rural Housing Service (RHS) and the programs are generally referred to by the section number under which they are authorized in the Housing Act of 1949.

When disasters occur, such as Hurricane Katrina, the USDA provides housing relief to residents of the affected areas in general and to affected participants in the various USDA rural housing programs. The relief can be placed in three broad categories: (1) relief for homeowners and homebuyers; (2) relief for apartment dwellers; (3) and relief for multi-family property owners. In general, USDA assistance is only available if funds from the Federal Emergency Management Agency (FEMA), the Small Business Administration, other agencies, or insurers are inadequate to meet the housing needs of affected rural residents.

RELIEF FOR HOMEOWNERS AND HOMEBUYERS

USDA has authority to finance the purchase or repair of single-family housing under Sections 502 and 504 of the Housing Act of 1949.

Section 502

Under the Section 502 program, qualified applicants may obtain loans for the purchase or repair of new or existing single-family housing in rural areas. Borrowers may either obtain direct loans from USDA or obtain loans from private lenders which are guaranteed by USDA.

Borrowers with income of 80% or less of the area median may be eligible for the direct Section 502 loans and may receive interest credit to reduce the interest rate to as low as 1%. The direct loans may be used to purchase existing homes, to repair homes that are already owned, or to construct new homes. Borrowers with income of up to 115% of the area median may obtain USDA-guaranteed loans from private lenders. Guaranteed Section 502 loans may only be used to purchase existing dwellings or to construct new homes. Priority is given to first-time homebuyers, and USDA may require that borrowers complete a homeownership counseling program.

Historically, about 98% of the loans have been used for home purchases. The homes to be financed must be "modest" in cost and design and must be located in rural areas serviced by the USDA. To be eligible for a Section 502 loan, a borrower must have the means to repay the loan but be unable to secure reasonable credit terms elsewhere.

After a presidentially-declared disaster, borrowers are eligible for a six-month moratorium on mortgage payments if they live in the disaster area and have direct Section 502 loans from the USDA. If necessary, the moratorium may be extended, but the moratorium may not exceed two years. Interest will continue to accrue on the unpaid loan balance during the moratorium. Upon resumption of scheduled payments the loan is to be re-amortized to include the amount deferred. After adjusting for any interest rate subsidy available to the borrower, all or part of the interest accrued during the moratorium may be forgiven to the extent that the new mortgage payment would exceed the borrower's ability to pay.

Borrowers whose homes have been damaged by the disaster may also be eligible for new Section 502 loans to pay for needed repairs.

The USDA has no direct control over the actions of lenders that participate in its housing programs. In cases of presidentially-declared disasters, the USDA sends a letter to lenders who hold USDA-guaranteed Section 502 loans, and asks that such lenders cease foreclosures and offer payment forbearance to Section 502 borrowers who live in the disaster areas.

Section 504

Under the Section 504 program, rural homeowners with incomes of 50% or less of the area median may qualify for USDA direct loans to repair their homes. The proceeds must be used to remove identified health and safety hazards or to remodel the dwellings to make them accessible and useable for household members with disabilities. Loans are limited to $20,000. Owners who are age 62 or more may qualify for grants of up to $7,500 to pay for the needed home repairs. To qualify for the grants, the elderly homeowners must lack the ability to repay the full cost of the repairs.

Depending on the cost of the repairs and the income of the elderly homeowner, the owner may be eligible for a grant for the full cost of the repairs or for some combination of a loan and a grant which covers the repair costs. The combination loan and grant may total no more than $27,500.

As with the Section 502 program, borrowers with Section 504 loans are eligible for a six-month payment moratorium if the mortgaged property is within a presidentially-declared disaster area. The loans are reamortized upon resumption of mortgage payments. Borrowers may also be eligible for new Section 504 loans to pay for damage caused by the disaster.

Rental Housing Preference as Displaced Tenants

Homeowners who are made homeless as a result of a presidentially-declared disaster, and who are borrowers under the Section 502 program (either direct or guaranteed) or the Section 504 program (either loans or grants), are eligible for occupancy nationwide as "displaced tenants" at any USDA-financed multi-family housing projects. They are given a letter of priority eligibility (LOPE), which moves them to the top of waiting lists for vacancies in other properties. The LOPE is good for 120 days. After 120 days the family may remain on the waiting list but without priority. An expedited placement process waives maximum income limits, security deposits, and credit checks; streamlines month-to-month leasing procedures; and institutes telephone background checks.

RELIEF FOR APARTMENT RENTERS

USDA has authority to finance multi-family housing under Sections 514, 515, 516, and 538 of the Housing Act of 1949. Section 521 of the act provides authority to offer rental assistance to low-income renters who reside in USDA-financed rental housing.

Section 515

Under the Section 515 program, USDA is authorized to make direct loans for the construction of rural rental and cooperative housing. Except for public agencies, all borrowers must demonstrate that financial assistance from other sources will not enable the borrower to provide the housing at terms that are affordable to the target population. The funds may also be used to buy and improve land and to provide necessary facilities such as water and waste disposal systems.

Section 514 and Section 516

Under the Section 514 program, USDA is authorized to make direct loans for the construction of housing and related facilities for farm workers. The loans are repayable in 33 years and bear an interest rate of 1%. Except for state and local public agencies or political subdivisions, the applicants must be unable to obtain financing from other sources that would enable the housing to be affordable by the target population. Under the Section 516 program, USDA is authorized to make grants of up to 90% of the development cost to nonprofit organizations and public bodies seeking to construct housing and related facilities for farm workers. Applicants must demonstrate a "pressing need" in the area for the housing and show there is reasonable doubt that it can be provided without the grant. The remaining 10% of the cost may be from the applicant's own resources, from other sources, or from Section 514 loans.

Section 521

Under the Section 521 program, the USDA is authorized to make rental assistance payments to owners of rental housing (Sections 515 or 514) to enable eligible tenants to pay no more than 25% of their income in rent. The rental assistance payments, which are to be made directly to the property owners, are to make up the difference between the tenants' payments and the USDA-approved rent for the units. Owners must agree to operate the property on a limited profit or nonprofit basis.

For residents receiving Section 521 rental assistance in units made uninhabitable by a presidentially-declared disaster, USDA permits the transfer of the rental assistance to another eligible Section 514 or Section 515 apartment complex. The transfer must be agreed to by all parties and be designed for the return of the residents and the rental assistance to the original complex and unit after the property has been restored. If the tenant chooses to stay instead of returning to the original complex, the tenant will not be assured rental assistance, and the owner would charge an appropriate rent based on any subsidy available to that property.

Section 538

Under the Section 538 program, borrowers may obtain loans from private lenders to finance multifamily housing, and USDA guarantees to pay for the lender losses in case of borrower default. Section 538 guaranteed loans may be used for the development costs of housing and related facilities that (1) consist of five or more adequate dwelling units, (2) are available for occupancy only by renters whose income at time of occupancy does not exceed 115% of the median income of the area, (3) would remain available to such persons for the period of the loan, and (4) are located in a rural area.

Rental Housing Preference as Displaced Tenants

Residents of Section 515 Section 514, Section 516 and Section 538 housing, who are made homeless as a result of a presidentially-declared disaster, are eligible for occupancy nationwide as "displaced tenants" at any USDA-financed multi-family housing projects. They are to be given a letter of priority eligibility (LOPE), which moves them to the top of waiting lists for vacancies in other properties. The LOPE letter is good for 120 days. After 120 days the family may remain on the waiting list but without priority. Documentation of being registered with FEMA may be used in lieu of a LOPE letter. An expedited placement process waives maximum income limits, security deposits, and credit checks; streamlines month-to-month leasing procedures; and institutes telephone background checks.

RELIEF FOR MULTI-FAMILY PROPERTY OWNERS

Owners of Section 514 and Section 515 properties in disaster areas are to be given a 90-day moratorium on mortgage payments. Applicants must meet two conditions to qualify: (1) have properties in the areas designated as disasters, and (2) provide verification that the damage to the property was a direct result of the disaster. At the end of the moratorium the loan may be reamortized, the loan may be refinanced, or USDA may enter a work-out plan with the borrowers.

The USDA is to send letters to lenders holding Section 538 loans, suggesting that the lenders offer similar forbearance to Section 538 borrowers in disaster areas.

LEGISLATION IN THE 109TH CONGRESS

The Rural Housing Hurricane Relief Act of 2005 (H.R. 3895), as passed by the House on October 6, 2005, would amend the Housing Act of 1949 to provide rural housing assistance to families affected by Hurricane Katrina or Hurricane Rita.

Section 541 of the National Housing Act provides that, in cases of presidentially-declared disasters, the USDA must allocate disaster assistance to affected states for use in counties designated as disaster areas and to counties contiguous to such counties. Allocations may be made over three fiscal years beginning on the date of the declaration. In general the funds may be used for any of USDA's authorized housing purposes. Local governments, their agencies, and nonprofit organizations may use the funds for the construction or rehabilitation of housing for agricultural workers.

As passed, H.R. 3895 would amend Section 541 such that it only applied to counties designated as disaster areas in connection with Hurricane Katrina or Hurricane Rita, counties contiguous to such counties, and individuals residing in these counties at the time of the disaster. For Section 514 or Section 515 properties in these areas that had been allocated Section 521 rental assistance, and which had become uninhabitable because of the disaster, the USDA would have the option of converting the Section 521 rental assistance into either Section 8 vouchers or rural housing vouchers. Affected tenants would be able to use the vouchers to pay towards the cost of renting substitute housing. The USDA would be permitted to use the vouchers in areas that do not meet the definition of "rural."

The bill would amend the rural housing voucher program (Section 542) by no longer limiting its use to very- low-income families, and permit its use by certain low-income families. Eligible low-income families would be those who reside or resided in areas that were subject to Presidential disaster declarations in connection with Hurricane Katrina or Hurricane Rita, and whose residences became uninhabitable or inaccessible as a result of these disasters. The limit of 5,000 rural housing vouchers in a fiscal year would not apply to vouchers authorized under these provisions.

The authority for the amended Sections 541 and 542 would apply during the six-month period beginning on the date of enactment of H.R. 3895.

As noted above, under present law Section 502 guaranteed loans may only be used for purchasing existing dwellings or constructing new homes. The bill would amend the law to provide that guaranteed loans may also be used to repair or rehabilitate existing properties in rural areas.

INDEX

D

E

S